CW01064190

A Plot to Deceive & Destroy Us:
A Demonic Agenda

DR. C.M. TEAGUE

Foreword By: Master Teague III

805 South Church Street, Suite 17,
Murfreesboro Tennessee 37130

Copyright © 2024 Overcome

ISBN: 9798330248506

Scripture was taken from the Holy Bible. ENGLISH STANDARD VERSION® (ESV®). Copyright ©: 2001 by Crossway. All rights reserved worldwide. NEW INTERNATIONAL VERSION® (NIV®) Copyright ©: 2024 by Biblehub.com.

Editor's Note

Yahweh and Yeshua

You will notice in this book the frequent use of the names Yahweh, when referring to God the Creator of all things and Yeshua, when referring to Jesus/Christ/Messiah. There are important reasons for that. First, Yahweh is the personal name of God and is native to Hebrew[3]. It is our desire as Christians to have a personal relationship with Yahweh as Abraham did and does. In addition, Yahweh is the most common Hebrew noun in the Bible. That being said, it seems appropriate and beneficial to use the personal name Yahweh in the context of discussing destructive personal attacks from the enemy. Secondly, the name Yeshua means "to save or to deliver" in the Hebrew language. It is this Power to save and deliver that helps us to see and respond to the enemies' deadly and destructive lies and schemes. It is this Power that restores our personal fellowship with Yahweh, which allows us to receive the blessings that were created for us[3].

A PLOT TO DECEIVE AND DESTROY US: A DEMONIC AGENDA

TABLE OF CONTENTS

A Plot to Deceive & Destroy Us: A Demonic Agenda

ACKNOWLEDGMENTS

I would like to acknowledge St. Paul of Tarsus for His obedience to what he was called to by our Lord and Savior Christ Yeshua. It is his guidance by the Holy Spirit in the letters written to the churches that open my eyes to the ever presence of deception and the proper Yahweh pleasing responses I am to have as a member of the Body of Christ, the Church.

Foreword
Written by Master W. Teague III

I wanted to take some time out to acknowledge this great body of work that you will soon digest through these pages. I am honored to not only be an early digester of this literature, but also the proud son of the author. It is a privilege to be a small part of one of his many books written. As a son that knows his father as a consistent and avid reader of the Word of God who has also been exposed to the gambit of life's experiences, his writings are not only grounded in truth, but also in testimony.

It is evident that this work "A Plot to Deceive and Destroy Us: A Demonic Agenda" is Holy Spirit filled and exemplary in identifying and extracting the schemes of our enemy and enemies to deceive and destroy the world and the Ambassadors of Christ. This book revealed to me the many angles at which the enemy does this through seemingly harmless ways of thinking, talking, and or being. I most certainly found myself convicted at certain moments as I came to realize a false way of thinking, talking, or being I've aligned myself with that truly is a lie of the enemy.

I have the upmost confidence in saying that as you read the pages of this book, you will be challenged to change some perspectives you have on what the enemy uses to deceive and how he uses it to deceive. Through the scripturally based and in-depth insight this book provides into how "your enemy the devil prowls around like a roaring lion looking for someone to devour, " rest assured you will become more "alert and of sober mind" as the scripture states in 1 Peter 5:8.

It is appropriate to mention that this book is not at all meant to evoke fright or fear in your life, but to strengthen you in the joy of the Lord, knowing that we have power over all the enemies' attempts to divert us from the righteous path. I have confidence that what the Lord has produced through my father will touch many more people than he imagined. This book is a must read for believers of our Lord to better understand the ways the enemy attempts to both deceive and destroy them and this world. May this book reach high and low and far and wide and touch all those God desires it to.

With support and admiration,

Master Teague III
Author of "The Power of Community At The Ohio State University: Shine God's Light, Make Kingdom Impact"

A Plot to Deceive & Destroy Us: A Demonic Agenda

INTRODUCTION

A Plot to Deceive and Destroy Us: A Demonic Agenda is inspired by C.S. Lewis's work called Screwtape Letters. In C.S. Lewis's book Wormwood is a more advanced demon who is assigned to instruct and guide a lower-level demon, by the name of Screwtape, in the art of deception. Wormwood shared, taught and supervised a very dark, deceptive and destructive agenda. I was able to identify how this agenda rings true in the lives of those who seek to be the People of God and followers of Jesus Christ. It is first true because it is what we find written in the Holy Scriptures. In Revelation 12:17 and 13:7 the enemy has been allowed to make war with man who keep the commandments of God and hold to the testimony of Jesus.

My goal is to share what I have been shown in the Holy Scriptures and in my life in order to help you be more aware and discerning when it comes to hidden tricks and lies of our unseen and spiritual enemies. The Holy Spirit is a must to be able to be successful in these battles. Pray that He joins you as you read what He has shown me so that you can read with understanding and the Power of God. I prayed every moment of my writing because your life and my life in time and in eternity is a serious matter, not to ever be taken lightly or for granted.

This attack on the People of God (i.e. God's children) is an attack on mankind. It is not that all of mankind are children of God. It is that the enemy will use all of mankind to attempt to accomplish his goal. This is an attack because the enemy only comes to lie, steal, and destroy if one is a child of God or not (John 10:10). He will use anyone he can to get the job done. I know that some might cringe at what I just said about not everyone being a child of God. This is one example of the persuasions and deceptions that the enemy has installed in the minds of many. We most become aware of and remember what is written in the Gospel of John 1:12. It is written, "Yet to all who did receive Him (Jesus Christ), to those who believed in his name, he gave the right to become children of God". Notice the word "become". So, the truth is that we become the children of God. It is not an automatic thing that happens. Yet many believe that all of mankind are the children of God. Just imagine how different our discernment, compassion, and actions would be if we lived totally mindful of this truth about who are the children of God. We believe that if we think of everyone as a child of God, we will love them better but that is a deception, and the opposite is true. If we understand that not everyone is a child of God, we will desire that for them and love them better in the way we engage them. Our convictions and our compassions would have no choice but to be steadfast and growing. We tend to leave people alone in their false joy and suffering and challenge them differently when we believe everyone is a child of God. It is an effective deception because it "feels right". It is a plot to destroy because it is not true.

We can also look at the famous Word of God in the verses of Psalm 23 ("The Lord is my Shepherd") to understand who the children of God are. Actually, you have to look at both Psalm 22 and 23. Psalm 23 is an extension of Psalm 22. Before you read Psalm 22, ask the Holy Spirit to allow you to see the suffering, praise and prosperity of the Messiah because that is what it shows. It is the faith and works of faith that is born out of the belief of Psalm 22 that allows us to be able to apply Psalm 23 to us or another person. A summation of these two wonderful chapters is that our Lord and Savior came to this earth, told us the truth, showed us the truth, laid down his life for us to have eternal life with Him and providing us with whatever we need to overcome this world. Unequal to Him is the enemy and the efforts of the enemy. The enemy is not opposed to good morals. He is opposed to: "The Lord is my Shepherd" and "Jesus is Lord". The enemy can manipulate good morals, but he cannot manipulate the presence of the Holy Spirit that always points to Jesus Christ (John 16:8-14). We in our imperfections are ripe for a plot that deceives and destroys.

THE ENEMY

CHAPTER I

A Broad Attack

The Word of God tells us that our battle is not with flesh and blood. Then who is our battle against? It surely seems like flesh and blood is the cause of our issues. What we must understand is what the Word of God continues to say about this battle. That is, our flesh and blood respond to a humanistic state of mind, intellectual strongholds, unGodly authorities, worldly things that we give lordship to and unholy spiritual influences (Ephesians 6:12). It is these things that are the root of the battle and God is trying to help us go to battle against the root not the fruit. Therefore, the root of the struggle is the devil and his demon's schemes as well as our very own fallen state.

Our enemies want to disguise themselves and their ways as different things. They want to hit us with attacks from one million different directions. This is why God tells us that the road to destruction is broad (Matthew 7:13). There are so many ways to get there. Until we mindfully understand this, we will be vulnerable to their attacks and in many situations not even know we have been attacked. These attacks then alter our course and pull us away from God the Father, God the Son and God the Holy Spirit. Our enemies will use philosophy and empty deception, which are based on human tradition and the spiritual forces of the world to take us captive (Colossians 2:8). They will use false science and distorted thinking connected to the desires of the flesh. They will also deny science and isolate theories in order to attack our intellect, emotions and habits. It is like being brainwashed into disobedience.

The enemy wants to distract you with many things. This is why God calls us to be sober minded, to renew our minds, look out for one another so we can remain focused on one thing and not rely on our own understanding (1 Peter 5:8; Romans 12:2; 1 Thessalonians 5:11; Proverbs 3:5). Only God's Holy Spirit can renew our minds and urge us to know and do the things that are pleasing to God. He is our Helper, and we must rely on what He reveals to us. He will not force it on us but if we seek and thirst for the Kingdom of God and His righteousness, Divine wisdom and strength will be given to us. We can also understand why He teaches us not to lean on our own understanding but to trust and submit to Him (Proverb 3:5-6). As humans we initially understand things based on our unreliable constructed memories that are based on our past and present personal experiences which are narrow understandings. Therefore, we really need God's understanding to truly understand the many different things we experience. Truth, righteousness, peace, faith, and salvation will be given to us when we lean on the understanding only He can give. These things are based on One person, Jesus Christ. This is why God tells us that the road is narrow that leads to life. There is only one way (John 14:6).

We want to have faith in this one Way. Believe it or not, but the enemy does not put a lot of stock in stopping you from having faith. What he hates is when your faith is contagious. For the enemy, seeking to cause no faith is good but improbable so isolated faith is his target. If he can keep us from "doing life" with each other he has won that battle. If he cannot keep us from each other, then to create noise is the next best thing to silence our faith and disturb our silence. The enemy loves noise. Noise can drown out a beautiful song of praise. Noise can invade our quiet time with the Lord. Noise can uplift a lie. It is the perfect weapon against the "good things", things to be grateful for, in our lives.

We must also be aware of our own and other people's minds and intellectual strongholds. These things are not flesh and blood either. They are unseen and invisible. We do battle with these things daily. We do battle with these things in other people and even within ourselves. Paul boldly proclaims that we are to tear down every argument that stands against the knowledge of God and that we are to capture every thought to make it obedient to the Word of God (2 Corinthians 10:5). This clearly points to state of minds and intellectual strongholds of others as wells as our state of mind. Hopefully we can understand how vast these things can be and therefore, how dangerously and unknowingly they can sneak into people's lives. These things are an enemy as well. These things are things that influence mankind's flesh and blood to do bad deeds. That is, deeds that God commands us not to do.

Temptation

The enemy wants to tempt you to sin, and he/it does. This deserves repeating so we will not forget this. The enemy wants to tempt you to sin, and he/it does. This is easier to do when we are feeling down, and he knows it. When we are stressed, we tend to want to relieve that stress and we can find ourselves using things that are not pleasing to God and even being idolatrous (replacing God…believing God is not enough). We can have evil thoughts and/or evil behaviors that seem to make us "feel" better. Using the word "evil" here is tricky because we have tremendously shortened the list of things that we consider to be evil in this world. We must broaden that list if we are to avoid being deceived and destroyed. We must understand and identify evil the way the Lord our God describes it. Yahweh tells us that His ways and His thoughts are not like ours as He has a higher standard (Isaiah 55:8-9). A tell-tell sign of a mature Christ Follower is the presence of a constant practice of discernment/distinguishing good from evil (Hebrews 5:14). Culture teaches us that many things are not evil, and that is just a big lie.

Our first nature is to think and do as our Creator designed us to think and do but there is a second nature that has emerged in us due to our fallen state. This second nature is one of the main reasons we can be tempted. We have heard people say things like, "It has become second nature" or "It is her second nature". We know second nature means that something has become almost natural, happening most of the time. It is not natural and that is why it is labeled "second". Bill Graham expressed that, "We have two natures within us, both struggling for mastery. Which one will dominate us? It depends on the one we feed". The enemy wants us to think, feel, and believe that evil is Spiritually natural when it is not. He wants us to feed our second nature. He wants to change our attitudes towards evil. Therefore, the enemy wants to increase our cravings for unnatural pleasure (second nature pleasure). This type of pleasure is pleasure that diminishes because it is unnatural. This is not how God intended pleasure to be which is why it is diminishing. It is not our first Spiritual nature. The enemy wants us to seek pleasure that diminishes because it will keep us in a vicious cycle of chasing that pleasure fix. It will keep us trapped in what we crave and not leaning on the One Who saves. We all can imagine those things that "feel good" in the moment but only last for the moment. Therefore, we find ourselves chasing that "feel good moment" again days, a day, or even hours later. This is what the enemy tempts us to do. He wants to condition us to associate pleasure with something unGodly. Once this conditioning happens, we become a slave to that diminishing pleasure. It controls us. We learn from the wisest person who ever lived that pleasure is meaningless and the entire responsibility of man is to respect and obey God (Ecclesiastes 2:1 and 12:13-14). We have an enemy who has an agenda to make sure the latter does not happen.

The enemy knows that unGodly pleasures do not sustain peace in our lives and pushes us farther from God, but for him, that is sometimes not enough. He wants to add novelty to the mix because he knows we are suckers for "new things". He knows that he can, not only tempt us, but also persuade us with novelty. It can be a new experience, new object, or a new idea. This novelty goes hand in hand with discontentment. He wants to tempt and persuade us with novelty inside or outside of our marriages and committed relationships, with the cars we drive, the causes we advocate for, the devices we use, and even ideas in our minds. He does not want us to be satisfied with anything. Either way, he is stacking persuasion alongside the temptation. The enemy wants us to desire novelty which diminishes pleasure. I hope we see how twisted this can be. The enemy wants us to seek unGodly pleasure so that we can experience that pleasure and like it. He knows that this pleasure diminishes on its own. However, he wants to sometimes cause already diminishing pleasure to diminish further by persuading us with novelty. He wants discontentment to grow in us as well as condition us to associate pleasure with something unGodly. We must guard our hearts and renew our minds (Proverbs 4:23 and Romans 12:2). This is a battle for our hearts and minds.

Persuasion

We must understand that persuasion runs deeper and more intellectual than novelty. The enemy has many weapons of persuasion. Persuasion is enticing. It tickles our habits, likes, and desires. There are two ways to persuade us. We can be persuaded with reason or emotionally[1]. We can guess which one the enemy will not be using. He wants to present you with jargon not reason (e.g. "A phrase" vs. what is true and false). The enemy wants to entice you with empty jargon and slogans that take advantage of our emotions. When our emotions are taken advantage of it makes us too dumb to interact in open dialogue or debate. We see this type of persuasion running ramped today. Slogans and jargon usually have nothing to do with the urging of the Holy Spirit and therefore are not faith-based. Most of the time, these things are manmade, man-initiated or man-imagined after enticement of the enemy or the indulgence of self. That means that God has no part in it. The children of God are not led by these things because we are led by the Holy Spirit, and this helps us to not delight in selfish exaltation (Romans 8:14 and Galatians 5:16). The enemy knows the selfish tendencies of our flesh and how it not only damages us but also those around us. He longs to incite pride and hatred.

The enemy wants to build this pride and hatred through faction (tribes, groups, division etc.). He will also use tribal jargon and tribal slogans to build pride and hatred. He starts with pride. He wants us to feel really good about ourselves personally regardless of our thoughts and behaviors and will put people in our life (in person or online) to affirm us. We know that pride of life is one of the three things that is not of God in this world (1 John 2:16). Once the enemy gets this pride of life to set in on us, he then can turn our attention to those who do not admire us like we think or feel we should be admired. He fools us into thinking that we just want to be accepted but truly we want to be admired. Now he has us in a position to develop hatred towards those who do not "accept" (i.e. admire) us. You see this deception and destruction in many aspects of life, but it is most obvious in regard to sex.

The enemy wants us to be misdirected when it comes to sexual taste. How does he misdirect us? He does it by ever shifting the social norms. He knows that people influence people. Take for example, homosexual behavior. He knows that the more people who approve of such behavior the more likely that more people will have such behavior. It will not matter that they do not truly have same-sex attraction or that they are not trying to have a homosexual identity. All that matters is that they are now okay with trying an act that might be pleasurable and seemingly approved by society. This process is also true of heterosexual behavior. In both situations, the enemy wants God's desires for us to become abnormal and the opposite to become normal. We are taught by the Holy Scriptures that we will sorrowfully regret considering good things to be evil and evil things to be good (Isaiah 5:20). We have an enemy who has an agenda to put us in that position. He has an agenda to make crooked our corruptible state of mind.

STATE OF MIND

CHAPTER II

Right or Wrong?

Many do not consider that their state of mind is vulnerable to attack. What and how we think about things can change over time for the better or for the worse. Most of the time if it changes for the worse, we are unaware of the distance our minds have traveled away from the Lord our God. We must pray that our awareness stays intact and that our minds are sealed by the Holy Spirit. The enemy does not want us to see things as true or false but as philosophical. A truckload of options is bound to have us lost wherever we land. That is, the enemy does not attack our minds with things that are obviously wrong. If he did, we could easily respond and defeat his attempts. The trick is to attack our minds with things that are "almost right". These types of lies take more motivation and effort to detect and are easier to defend if we choose them. He knows that if we chose something that is "almost right", we can easily fool ourselves to think and feel it is right. The truth that we must stay focused on is that "almost right" is wrong and "almost true" is false. The Word of Yahweh warns us of this through St. Paul when he said, "You were running the race so well. Who has held you back from following the truth? It certainly isn't God, for he is the one who called you to freedom. This false teaching is like a little yeast that spreads through the whole batch of dough! I am trusting the Lord to keep you from believing false teachings. God will judge that person, whoever he is, who has been confusing you." (Galatians 5:7-10). The enemy may go even farther and jam us up with "almost right" things. That is, he wants to have almost right things to come into our lives often, frequently and one after the other, back to back. If he does, he is trying to shorten the time we have to detect a lie before he presents another lie. He wants us to make a hasty decision about what to think, which will more than likely end up in us believing a lie or ignoring a lie. This combination of "almost rights" and a truck load of back-to-back "almost rights" attacks our ability to renew our minds, think clearly and gain awareness of the truth. Russian Grand Chess Master, Casperoff, said, "The point of modern propaganda is not only to misinform or push an agenda, it is to exhaust your critical thinking so as to annihilate truth". However, we may gain awareness of a lie and not believe it to be true. Either way, the enemy wants us to put a lot of personal effort in believing what we believe (true or false...right or wrong). He longs to see this personal effort from us because he wants us to think that we know it all. The more we are prideful in our investment in a lie or the truth the greater the chance we may become a "know it all". The enemy knows that a "know it all" ruins relationships as well as contaminates the truth with his or her pride. This is a win-win situation for the enemy. He has created a philosophical "know it all" who believes they are just simply defending what is true or what is right when what they are defending is only something that is almost true or almost right or something that is true, drowned out by the noise of their pride. C.H. Spurgeon said, "Wisdom is the right use of knowledge. To know is not to be wise. There is no fool so great as the knowing fool. But, to know how to use knowledge is to have wisdom." The enemy wants us to misuse things that are almost right and therefore wrong, as well as misuse things that are actually right.

Rendered Ineffective

This life offers many opportunities for us to positively affect a great number of people, directly or indirectly. We start to have a self-concept about our character driven virtues very early in our lifespan. We grow to somewhat be aware of our virtues and the benefit our virtues can be to others. The people's lives we can benefit the most is usually someone we have access to locally. However, the enemy understands our weakness towards the pride of life that 1 John 2:16 warns us about. He hopes to influence a state of mind in which we do not dream of helping our neighbor right in front of us, but doing something we think is bigger than that. The enemy wants to make our virtues more like fantasy by imaging them being applied abroad rather than in our sphere of influence. This puts us in the posture of spending a lot of time with our imaginations about the things we can do as opposed to acting on the things we can do. The personal and communal adventures, that God calls us to, start right in front of us. We do not truly connect with our virtues on a realistic personal level if we only attempt to connect with our virtues imagining using them in some grand impersonal manner. Over time we can even start to question if we have such virtues at all if we get stuck in imaging things as opposed to doing things. Once the questioning starts the efforts dwindle. This is what the enemy wants. He wants our character driven virtues to get stuck in our imaginations because there they will be fruitless and not a part of reality. We destroy our opportunities to be a neighbor to our neighbors and our enemies when we think too big and isolate ourselves to only our imaginations. It becomes a huge barrier to us sharing the Truth and Love of Christ right where we are.

It takes a level of courage to narrow our focus to go to work for the Lord. It takes a level of courage to accomplish many things in our lives. Courage can be described as a state of mind that becomes a state of action (i.e., work of the hands). God is not pleased when we lack courage because faith requires action in many life experiences. Therefore, the lack of courage can lead to wickedness. Revelation 21:8 tells us that "the cowardly" along with others "will be consigned to the fiery lake of burning sulfur". Therefore, courage is more than important. The enemies that stand against Yeshua want to remove our courage so that wickedness can then grow, the wickedness of low expectation, hope, faith, and willpower. The enemy wants us to broaden our fear focus instead of realistically narrowing it. This will paint a picture that lies about the presence, number, and magnitude of things to fear. The enemy wants us to believe that many things are against us which warrants running away from hope. We then run away from Yahweh given opportunities and experiences that glorifies His blessings and all sorts of grace that He provides. Proverbs 28:1 teaches us the "The wicked flee when no one pursues, but the righteous are bold as a lion". We flee from things that are not even to be feared. We flee from fears that do not even exist when we listen to the lies of the enemy.

If we can overcome the false fears of the enemy, the battle is far from over for him and therefore for us. He will then want our causes to become our religion and for us to value our faith through the lens of the "cause", not the "cause" through the lens of our faith especially if the cause is not born of the Holy Spirit. Therefore, he wants us to worship our cause and not our Yahweh, which goes against the first and greatest commandment. The first commandment in the Ten Commandments is, "You shall have no other gods before me" (Exodus 20:3). The enemy wants to deceive us to do so. Take for instance, "worldly social justice". It is not born of the Holy Spirit and many of us have lifted it up higher than we have lifted up Christ Himself. If the Word of God does not align with "worldly social justice" we will twist His commands to fit into "worldly social justice" or simply ignore Him. What we should do is amend "worldly social justice" to fit into the Word of Yahweh. Bye the way, Yahweh has a lot to say about social justice and you can find it in Exodus 22:16-31 and 23:1-9. This is what we use to focus on and start any social justice deeds. We must use the Word of Yahweh to test all causes (1 John 4:1). However, the enemy would rather we warp our state of mind and worship the created, not the Creator which goes against the warning we have received (Romans 1:25). The end result is the corruption of a good cause and the practice of idolatry. There is no worship or power of Yahweh in that position and that is what the enemy wants.

Twisted Priorities

What are your priorities as a Child of Yahweh, a Christ follower? Hopefully we can answer this question by saying, "His priorities are my priorities". Learning His priorities comes with seeking His righteousness. Yeshua tells us, "Blessed are those who hunger and thirst for righteousness, they shall be filled (Matthew 5:6). The Psalmist shares his satisfaction in righteousness and says, "As for me, I behold thy face in righteousness: I shall be satisfied, when I awake, with thy likeness". His righteousness in us leads to us being like Him and therefore having His priorities. These priorities get twisted by our fallen human nature and the enemy. How does this happen. One way is that the enemy wants us to be flippant (indifferent) in your humor. What does that mean? It means that He wants us to use humor as a vehicle for unrighteous thoughts, behavior, and language. He wants us to see indecent, immoral things packaged in humor as neutral, not good, or bad. Secondly, the enemy wants us to be flippant in our choice of music. He also wants us to use music as a vehicle for unrighteous thoughts, behavior, and language. Sometimes I get people to write down the words of their favorite song or two on a piece of paper. After that, I get them to read the words, not sing or rap, but read them aloud to themselves. Finally, I ask them to find their child or a child they know and read the song to them. I know before they get to that final step, they will already be shocked, concerned, or convicted by simply reading the song aloud to themselves. Humor and music can cause us to bracket our values. This bracketed state of mind is simply misplaced, and we lose sight of different things that please God and enrich our relationship with Him. Unfortunately, indifferent humor is not the only type of humor that twists up our priorities. The enemy also wants you to use humor to cover shameful acts (using humor as an excusing grace). A person might speak humorously about being disrespectful to someone else or even their infidelity. The enemy finds victory in this because he has gotten the person to treat practiced sin lightly and because the person tends to do this with an audience of at least one other person. If that other person starts to belittle the practiced sin in his or her heart as well, the enemy then has killed two or more birds with one stone. One person using humor to cover shameful acts has now contaminated one or more people with the same state of mind. It does not end there. Now the enemy may have the humor originating person in a position to lie as well if his shameful behavior continues and is of the nature of being a secret to be kept from someone else. The enemy wants you to keep up external behaviors as a Christian (appearances) and to feel there is no need to repent. This is where the shame covering humor will lead us to. Once we are in this position, the enemy hopes that we continue to spiral downward. In order to hold on to the need not to repent, he knows we need more than humor. We must ignore Yahweh. The enemy wants to increase your reluctance to think about Yahweh, at least in a certain area of our life. It is usually in the area where the humor is applied. Once we start to ignore Yahweh in certain areas, we still will engage Him in other areas. This is not good because this is what the enemy wants. The enemy wants you to not omit but dislike our religious duties. Our Lord warns us that we cannot serve two masters, because we will hate one and love the other (Matthew 6:24). The enemy is betting that we will hate our Lord and Savior and hold fast to our cherished sin and unrepentant double-minded state of mind. As this continues, the enemy knows this will cause you to have unreality and inattention in your prayers. How does this happen? The cherished sin and unrepentant double-minded state of mind causes the Christian to start to exist in something like a fantasy land. It is a fantasy state of mind that causes the Christian to ignore the reality of their state of mind and omit seeking Yahweh's help in their prayers.

The enemy finally wants to sink you into dullness. This dullness blocks our motivation to enrich our relationship with our Lord and Savior. It holds us at a dangerous distance from Him. It can destroy our mindfulness of priority, and the presence of joy and peace in our lives and the enemy is hoping it is contagious.

Distorted Pleasure

Our state of mind about pleasure is very vulnerable. This is simply because there are competing authorities and experiences that are deceptive. One competing authority is society itself. Another challenge is our flesh itself. The enemy does not want you to feel genuine Godly sorrow or genuine Godly pleasure. Many of us have heard the saying, "A moment on the lips brings a lifetime on the hips". We can look at that statement in a concrete way and understand it to mean that if we seek pleasure from unhealthy food or too much food in the moment, we will not have long-lasting pleasure from that decision. That is the type of pleasure that the enemy wants us to seek and have. We can also look at that statement in an abstract way and understand it to mean that if we seek any pleasure just for the moment it can have a negative effect for a lifetime. This too is the type of pleasure the enemy wants us to seek and have. This type of pleasure seeking keeps us going back to something that we believe brings us true pleasure when it does not. Genuine Godly pleasure does not cause us to create unhealthy habits or addictive behaviors or minds. It does not cause us to make idols of things. It does not cause us to rely on things and substances to bring us peace (shalom). Yeshua told the Samaritan woman at the well that if she drinks of the water that He has, she will never thirst again (John 4:1-13). The waters that the enemy wants us to drink lead us to life-long thirsting and therefore make us a slave to false thirst quenchers, false pleasures. The enemy wants us to chase pleasures that are not the way God wants us to have pleasures. That is right. God does want us to enjoy things that He made pleasurable, and He knows the most pleasurable ways to do it.

Many Christians are deceived to believe that what is pleasing to God is never as pleasurable as what the world has to offer. We fall for this simply because we are fallen. What is more pleasurable, having sex before marriage or waiting and having sex for the first time after marriage? What is more pleasurable, going further into and living affirmed gender confusion or coming out of explored gender confusion? What is more pleasurable, using a drug to relieve stress or renewing your mind with the Word of Yahweh to relieve stress? What is more pleasurable, cursing at or gossiping about someone who has angered you or controlling your tongue? We could ask many more "What is more pleasurable" questions here. The enemy wants our state of mind to seek pleasure in the moment not pleasure that goes far beyond the moment.

One way the enemy interferes with our genuine Godly pleasures is to deceive us into thinking that they are foolish. Another way the enemy interferes with our genuine Godly pleasures is to deceive us into thinking that it is not normal (the norm) and normal is what we should want to be. He wants our pleasures to be strongly connected to preconventional wisdom or conventional wisdom. Preconventional wisdom (hedonism) is false wisdom that is connected to our instinctual desires to seek pleasure and avoid pain, and it says if we feel a certain way and have desires those things are our true selves and we should engage those feeling and desires[1]. Conventional wisdom (approval motive) is false wisdom that is connected to the social norms of the day and says that we should go along with what most people think and do or what is said or thought to be what most people think and do[1]. For instance, he wants us to believe that waiting for marriage to be sexually active is foolish because it is not normal. Which one is more pleasurable, having sex in the freedom of a loving, giving, loyal, deep, life-long, committed marriage with no chance for sexual disease, hurt and premature investment and very little chance of chronic confusion or having sex in the confines of a selfish fulfilling, questionable, shallow, short-term, uncommitted relationship or moment with increased sexual disease, confusion, hurt and premature investment. The earlier is genuine God pleasures and the other is deceptive and destructive pleasures from the enemy. One is long lasting, free, and peaceful, while the other is short-lived, costly, and burdensome. Out of all the married couples that I have counseled, I have never counseled a married couple in which both the man and woman were virgins when they married who struggled in their sex life or whose sex life threatened their marriage. However, I have counseled many married couples in which either the man or the woman or both the man and the woman were not virgins when they married who did struggle in their sex life or whose sex life threatened their marriage. I focus this moment so much on sex because sex has destroyed more peace and more lives than poverty or oppressive ethnocentrism (what some would call racism which is a deception itself because there is only one race but many ethnicities) since the beginning of the sexual revolution. However, there are many more other pleasures that the enemy distorts for our downfall.

The pleasures of the tongue are very complex and vary from moment to moment. The enemy wants us to find "in the moment pleasures" that require speaking and in the moment pleasures that require not speaking. Therefore, he wants us to shut up when we should not and to speak when we should not, and he wants to attach false pleasure to both types of moments. Both moments require a lack of self-control, which is one of the fruits of the Spirit (Galatians 5:22-23). Therefore, we need the Holy Spirit to help us tame our tongue because by ourselves we cannot as God warns us in the book of James. As Christians who seek to be led by the Holy Spirit, we all have experienced moments in which we were led in a certain way regarding our words and chose to do the opposite of how we were being led. Every time we do this, we feel pleasure in the moment, some sort of relief, but later we have no long-lasting genuine God pleasure but only regret. How do the enemy and our fallen nature keep us stuck in these regretful patterns? If moments are a test from God or not, the enemy hopes we do not have courage enough to do what we are led to do and hopes that we never experience enough long-lasting pleasure in doing what we are led to do that would motivate us to respond to being led. This is accomplished by sowing seeds of doubt. Doubt causes anxiety and we seek to relieve anxiety which can lead us to being stuck in the moment only aware of our selfish anxiety. On the other hand, when we have a strong and courageous state of mind that does not lean on our own understanding and we are led to speak or not speak, it may be difficult in the moment but in the long run we experience the pleasure of being obedient, righteously victorious, and therefore accurate. We have no regrets. A courageous and humble state of mind gives the enemy a formidable opponent, but he still has his hope and tricks to deceive us even when these are present.

Rogue Humility

The enemy prefers pride over humbleness. He wants you to be arrogant no matter what you believe. It is easier for him to deceive and destroy us if he can get us to have pride. He does not want us to be humble, but he cannot keep us from being that way. However, if you are humble, he wants to get you to be proud of your humbleness. Humbleness is the opposite of arrogance and pride. It is akin to meekness. Therefore, it is not the absence of the ability to be autonomous, have a degree of willpower or have a degree of initiative. It is the state of mind to desire to harness those characteristics to allow someone (Yahweh) bigger than us to influence us and the situations we encounter. The enemy knows that it is easy for us to feel good about ourselves after we do something that we intend to do and being successful at being humble is no different. The enemy wants us to go beyond humbleness and into a state of mind that is passive. This is what happens when we get prideful about being a humble person. This pride causes us to focus mostly on ourselves more than discerning the situation. We become passive to maintain our so-called pride but think that we are being humble. We cross over from being meek to being weak and ineffective for our Lord. A Christian cannot be a warrior for Christ if he begins to mistakes being passive as being humble. The enemy does not want this rogue state of mind about humility to stop here. The enemy hates you and wants you to hate yourself. Therefore, in the case of your humility, he wants you to see your humility as self-hatred. So how does it become that rogue? You must understand the mechanism and outcome of things that are false. As mentioned before, a Christian can go beyond humbleness into a state of mind that is passive. The Christian now has false humility when that happens. People who live out something that is false that they believe to be true, they will soon experience the falseness of their state of mind but still may not identify this experience as the process and outcome of a false belief. This is a subtle and unpleasant experience and if the person does not consciously identify or denies the source of this stress, they may start to experience a level of self-hatred. Pretense due to pride always ends in self-hatred, at least as a state of mind.

Stuck in The Past and The Future

There are four (4) levels of existence that are a part of the human experience. These are the past, the present, the future, and eternity. Mentally, where do you spend most of your time and efforts? Think about it. Where do most people tend to spend most of their time and effort mentally? The enemy does not want you to look to the present or eternity but wants you to look to the past and the future, especially the future because it is least like eternity. Why? There are three main reasons. One, the most important level is eternity. Two, the level that is mostly connected to eternity is the present. Three, the only level that is not promised is the future. If he does find us focusing on the present, he will then want the present focus mind-set to be connected to the future or the past; the past, because if we get stuck there, we will have no growth in the present time, or we will become obsessed about trying to make our future look different than our past. The enemy wants you to put faith in the future because that is putting faith in something you may not see. Also, the enemy knows that putting too much hope in the future, apart from eternity, may cause us to break commands, which is a form of greed, to achieve that hope. Yeshua teaches us using parable of the rich man with an abundant harvest and warns us of the dangers of putting too much faith and worry in the future (Luke 12:15-23). The Christian with a present-eternity state of mind will have no need to focus on the past due to repentance and forgiveness and no need to worry about the future because seeking His righteous in the present with eternity in mind leaves little room to doubt the future that may come or not.

Sex Exalted

Yahweh created sex and He shares with us and shows us in His word all the wonderful blessings that come from engaging sex the way He intended. He also shares with us and shows us all the negative consequences and curses that come from participating in sex the way He did not intend. People are more important than sex, while at the same time our sex is a human experience. Sex is resistible. Love is not sex. Also, your sexual urges are not who you are and therefore you do not have to live out your urges to be your true self. However, the enemy wants you to dehumanize sex or see "love" as irresistible and intrinsic. He wants us to see sex as more important than people or see sexual urges as "love". When he and our lust get us to desire sex more than we desire the person, we are dehumanizing that person. Many people say, "love is love" but what many people really mean is "sex is love" and therefore should not be resisted because it is part of our core. This state of mind comes directly from deception (self-deception and enemy deception).

Love in a romantic relationship is not the passion you feel towards someone but the exclusive lifelong commitment you are willing to devote yourself to. The truth is passionate feelings peak fast and then decrease over time in romantic relationships[1]. Passionate feelings do not disappear, just decrease. A healthy marriage does maintain a healthy level of passion even after it decreases. However, it will decrease. The good thing is that commitment and companionate love grows over time in healthy relationships[1]. However, the enemy wants you to desire and have sexual taste for something that does not exist. He can introduce these fantasies about sex in different ways over time. They can be introduced to us through culture, pornography, memories of past sexual experiences, media and/or other forms of entertainment.

The Terminal Drop

The enemy wants to darken your intellect. Your intellect is your capacity for knowledge, reasoning and understanding. He does this by encouraging us to direct our love towards the wrong thing, while influencing our arrogance to increase. Misdirected love is false love, which interferes with our capacity to gain true knowledge (wisdom). Arrogance is the opposite of humility, and the lack of humility interferes with our capacity to for reasoning. This lack of true knowledge and reasoning keeps us away from understanding. The most noticeable occurrence of this darken intellect in the modern and postmodern society is found in the anti-science community, the LGBTQIA2S+ community, the anti-Christ community and communities that have ethnocentrism. When people are near physical death there tends to be a significant drop in their intellect[2]. This can be said for Spiritual death as well. When people have a significant drop in their intellect they are near Spiritual death. We look at things backwards but believe that we are forward thinking.

Mine!!!!!!

The enemy wants you to have a strong sense of ownership (i.e., my, mine). This is not ownership that is connected to a responsible state of mind. It is ownership that is connected to a "my will" and "my strength" state of mind. We can place the word "my" in front of so many things: my house, my sex life, my job, my children, my decision, my money, my body and even my rights. A strong sense of ownership is not the same as a wise and responsible sense of ownership. A strong sense of ownership can cause us to become atheists in different areas of our lives. We think and live as if Yahweh does not exist in those areas. Therefore, we develop the attitude that we can do whatever we want to do or avoid whatever we find difficult, challenging, or fearful. The enemy wants our strong sense of ownership to deny Yahweh. He then wants our strong sense of ownership to turn into entitlement or comfort seeking. Comfort seeking turns into irresponsibility. Entitlement grows into envy. Envy grows into covetousness. Covetousness grows into hatred.

Spiritual Pride

Our Spiritual connection allows us to have growth and maturity in our faith. The enemy is fine with growth if pride enters the picture. The enemy wants you to have spiritual pride. As we grow in our faith, we overcome and accomplish different things in this world. Then we develop a Spiritual/faith self-concept. Spiritual pride will cause us to attempt to protect our past growth from harm just like we sometimes try to protect our self-esteem from harm. The Word of Yahweh warns us not to think too highly of ourselves (Romans 12:3). However, when we do, we put ourselves in a state of mind to protect past growth by ignoring or avoiding further opportunities for growth that include challenges or seem threatening to our Spiritual self-concept. Spiritual pride causes us to fear future inevitable failures that would lead to more growth. This state of mind posture will cause us to engage Scripture and our relationship with Christ and fellow Christians in a shallow way. Many start to say, "I have a relationship not a religion". Basically, they are saying, "I believe in God, but not His Word in my life". If we have Spiritual pride, we can and will manipulate and not speak truthfully about our relationship with Him because that is something we can control, but we know we cannot control His Word. Therefore, we treat His Word like the world does and simply call it religion, as if religion is evil. Once Spiritual pride settles in, the enemy then wants you to neglect the relevant holy and righteous questions and ask worldly ones. We will even start to "cherry pick" Scripture to answer questions to protect our past faith accomplishments (Spiritual self-concept) and our present worldly thoughts or activities which block further maturity. The enemy enjoys this because he also wants you to plan worldly things in with your Christianity. Spiritual pride and the aforementioned outcomes of it are the catalyst to this "worldly Christianity". Now we find ourselves just where the enemy wants us. He does not want you to be content in your faith. Worldly Christians are not content in their faith and become lukewarm, which would mean that, in the end, they are not Christians at all.

To Pray or Not to Pray

We spend most of our time in a waking state[1]. What does that mean? That simply means that our minds wander (i.e., daydream) often. Our minds wander when we are talking to people, watching television, listening to a speech, eating a meal, listening to music, at work etc. We can drive somewhere and not remember the trip once we arrive at our destination, because of mind wandering. We spend a lot of time wandering away from our conscious awareness. We do this for different reasons. We do it to escape a boring situation, to escape a stressful situation, to plan future events (near or far), and to imagine future events (near or far; pleasant or unpleasant). The enemy does not want your wandering mind to become subject to prayer. He does not want you to invite the power of Yahweh into stressful situations, future planning or your imagination about the future. He wants these frequent mind wandering moments to be self-indulgent. However, if prayer does become a part of our mind wandering, the enemy is not finished with his deception tactics. He then wants you to intellectualize your prayers and see outcomes as physical not Spiritual, leading to the thought that praying is not needed. He wants you to establish that only physical facts are real and Spiritual ones are subjective and therefore not as trustworthy. That is, we began to rely on our and other's logic and efforts (i.e., what we can clearly make sense of) as we wait and/or see our prayers responded to by Yahweh. Yahweh's responses to our trust in Him gets lost in our human intellect. We begin to see other Christians' testimonies highlighting Yahweh's response as questionable and even disputable. Therefore, we begin to put faith in the physical only and do not see how the physical points to the Spiritual or how the Spiritual explains the physical. We move from faith to idolatry. As we hold on to this idolatry, we get further away from being connected to our Yahweh's religion (precepts, standard, statues etc.). The enemy smiles at this because he wants you to feel like religion is a fantasy in the face of trouble or crisis.

An Aging Crisis

The enemy wants you to be prideful in your ageing. He knows that it takes time for people to become worldly self-centered, especially in connection with our successes. Therefore, the longer we are alive, the more time the enemy has to get us into a state of mind that believes our successes are our own doing. This pride can happen at different ages but typically after some long-term success. This type of pride presents itself in two different ways. The first way is obvious. He wants us to think we ourselves are not "in the world" but "of the world" in our success. An "of the world" state of mind sees the world as sort of a heavenly throne. No one can tell us different about our self-made cleverness, skills, ability, or good decision-making in this world system. We might even take ownership of success that was actually a team effort. The second way that we become prideful in our aging is not so obvious. Some even call it imposter syndrome. Not everyone with imposter syndrome is prideful, but many are, so beware. On the surface this looks like the person is not prideful due to their self-doubt. When we pull back the layers of the struggle with imposter syndrome, the person typically never has a state of mind that considers that their success is due to blessings of Yahweh. They have the imposter syndrome struggle because their state of mind is attempting to take all of the credit for their success in the world. They struggle with taking the credit for their success only because they refuse to see or have been deceived not to see that what they have is what they have received not just achieved. They would be able to have peace and overcome imposter syndrome if they could come to the truth that they do not have to take all the credit for their success because they are not the one to give all the credit to.

Fearful Hatred

The enemy wants you to have hatred with fear. UnGodly fear strengthens hatred. The enemy accomplishes this easier with the sufferings of others as opposed to our own suffering. He wants you to hate with the belief that who you hate is someone else's enemy and that someone else is a victim (hate on someone else's behalf). If he is successful in this, he gets a big victory in you, because he would have gotten your state of mind to be fearful, full of hate and unforgiving at the same time. We tend to become allies to those who we believe need some sort of assistance or those we believe are wrongfully suffering because of the minds and hands of someone else. When we can directly see the suffering of someone else but cannot directly experience the resilience or healing of that person, it makes it more difficult to pardon the perpetrator. If your friend or child gets betrayed in marriage, if you think someone you admire for whatever reason is being mistreated or wronged, if you believe a group of people are wrongfully suffering due to one person or another group of people, you will more than likely find it difficult to forgive. Not only that but you will mentally be in a position to develop fear of the perceived perpetrator in relation to the perceived victim. This unforgiving and fearful state of mind solidifies and hardens hatred (hatred on someone else's behalf). The enemy uses this state of mind to attempt to divide people for the long-term in people seeking righteous in the body of Christ. This state of mind leads to unrighteous suffering, which the enemy loves to see.

The Coward (I)

The enemy wants you to be a coward. Why? Think about it. Without courage you cannot form and maintain any virtuous characteristic in your life. It takes courage to have love, joy, kindness, goodness, faithfulness, gentleness, and self-control. It takes courage to rejoice in the truth to those that hate the truth. It takes courage to tear down false beliefs, feelings and actions that stand against the Word of Yahweh. It takes courage to deny yourself. It takes courage not to conform to worldly things. It takes courage not to rejoice at wrongdoing. It takes courage to be patient and kind. It takes courage to not envy others. It takes courage to not be arrogant. It takes courage to not insist on your own way. It takes courage to not be resentful. It takes courage to not be ashamed of the Gospel. It takes courage to go and make disciples.

The enemy wants us to lack courage, but he does not want us to become aware of our lack of courage in prayer and leaning on our Lord. He wants our lack of courage to become despair. In despair, we are more likely to grasp at anything to be our support, our reasoning, our knowledge giver, and our understanding. In despair, we become adulterous idolaters. One of my favorite verses in all Scripture is Joshua 1:9. Read it and believe it!

WORK OF THE HANDS
CHAPTER III

Faith Without Works

Christians have Yahweh pleasing intentions. However, not living out those intentions is a major error regarding the "work of our hands". We just discussed how our state of mind is under attack. We must also be aware of how the work of the hands is under attack as well. Salvation is the outcome we seek. Scripture tells us to work out our own salvation knowing that Yahweh works in us if we confess Yeshua Christ (Philippians 2:12). What better way to attempt to destroy Christians' salvation than to disrupt one of the vehicles that gets them there. That vehicle, alongside faith, is repentance. The enemy does not want you to convert repentance to action. There are two parts to repentance: the change of mind and the change of works (i.e., behavior). Repentance is to turn your mind and your behavior towards Yahweh and away from lust, desire, and pride that lead to sin, iniquity and transgression. If we have the mind and therefore intentions to repent but we do not change our behavior, we have fallen short. It is not that we cannot recover but the enemy does not want us to recover. He wants us to stay in the pattern of accomplishing the intension (i.e., repenting with our words) but not following it up with action. If he can get us to this point it can cause us to attempt to change what we believe or feel (intentions) to fit the unchanged behavior. What would this look like? We will more than likely do one of two things that will please the enemy. One, we could stop repenting in our minds and with our words (audible or inaudible) all together due to feeling helpless about behavior change that would indicate overcoming the sin, iniquity or transgression. Two, we could change or modify our beliefs and feelings about the sin, iniquity or transgression to match the unchanged behavior. However, there is a chance that we will eventually change the behavior to line up with our beliefs and feelings if we hold fast to them. Our goal is to change to align ourselves with Yahweh's Holiness and be persistent if we struggle with that change.

Stuck in The Past and The Future

It was shared in chapter two that there are four (4) levels of existence that are a part of the human experience. These are, the past, the present, the future and eternity. In chapter two, the question was asked, "Mentally, where do you spend most of your time and efforts?" The answer to that question is a great predictor of how we will answer this next question. Behaviorally, where is most of your time and efforts centered? More than likely your behavior will be parallel to your state of mind (mental processes). This is what the enemy wants if he has already gotten what he wants in regards to you not looking to the present or eternity but looking to the past and the future, especially the future because it is least like eternity. Remember, he wants you to put faith in the future because that is putting faith in something you may not see. Then we will have works only with our future in mind. A planned future that is set apart from eternity may cause us to break commands to achieve that hope. We would then be trying to build treasures on earth that will perish. We might even perish before we finish building that treasure or before we can enjoy it.

Past focused behavior is usually due the desire to change something that took place in the past. The truth is, we cannot change anything that happened in the past unless we are indirectly correcting a false memory that we have or lie that we were told. Therefore, focusing on the past to change the past is futile. The enemy also wants you to focus on the past to change the present and the future. This is because he knows we tend to do what we do not stop thinking about. Therefore, if we are too focused on the past to change the present and the future, we will not change the present and future at all. This is the ironic error that occurs when we attempt mind and behavior control in that way. If you sit and say to yourself, "I do not want to think about a pink elephant", what do you end up doing? If you sit and say to yourself, "I do not want to parent like my parents parented", what do you end up doing? I have had clients who were so focused on the past and not wanting to parent their child like their parents parented them that they ended up parenting like they were parented. 2 Corinthians 5:17 teaches us a great and wonderful truth as it says, "Therefore, if anyone is in Christ, he is a new creation. The old has passed away; behold, the new has come." If we seek to parent or to do anything with eternity in mind, we will automatically not parent or do something in a way we are trying to avoid. Therefore, focusing on what we want instead of what we do not want will correct the ironic mind control error and allow us to be present and eternity focused. It will train and help us to trust that Yahweh will take care of the future by preparing us how He sees fit. Also, the enemy knows that if we focus on the past, we will more than likely find it more difficult to forgive others and even ourselves.

Deadly Betrayals

The enemy literally comes to steal, kill and destroy! There is a saying that I like to say. I am not sure if it is my own, but I do not remember hearing it from anyone else. However, I like to say, "Give the Devil an inch and he will kill you". He will at least attempt to lead you to death. We know that death has lost its sting for those who are in Yeshua (Jesus) the Christ (Hosea 13:14; 1 Corinthians 15:55-56). Even so, it does not stop the enemy from wanting death for us. He wants death anyway he can get it. He even wants you to have tragic adulteries that lead to suicide or murder that come from the belief that love is irresistible. In chapter two under the heading "Sex Exalted" we discussed how the enemy "wants us to see sexual urges as "love" and therefore intrinsic and irresistible". Therefore, if we tragically end up committing adultery, he wants this twisted sense of love to exist in us and end with the crooked and wicked transgression of murder in order to have what we "cannot resist" or end with the crooked and wicked sin of suicide because you cannot have what we "cannot resist". I have seen too many stories in crime documentaries that left me with the question, "Why did he or she have to murder their spouse or have their spouse murdered?" This murderous or suicidal desire could come from the cheating spouse or the person the spouse is cheating with if either is experiencing this deceptive "irresistible love" and believes something, or someone is in the way of it.

Where Did the Time Go?

In time, time is one of the most important things we have. Many say, "Time flies when you are having fun". However, for so many people, time flies no matter what. One piece of "wisdom" I attempt to leave my students every semester is "Make every day the longest day of your life". There are different reasons to attempt to do this but the one I want to focus on is related to increasing the probability that we will be mindful of ourselves and others. I want to focus on this one because the enemy does not want you to inspect what you do with your time. Too many of us live an implicit life, which means that how we are influenced and what we think and what we do is hidden, even from ourselves because we are simply minimally conscious of it. If we are minimally conscious of our time, we can easily be influenced by things that are ungodly. If we are minimally conscious of our time, we are more than likely not living out the purpose and plan of our Lord God. If we live long lives, in the end, we do not want to say, "Where did time go?". We want to be able to say, "I have fought the good fight, I have finished the race, and I have remained faithful." (2 Timothy 4:7). We will be able to say this if we have faithfully inspected what we have done with our time.

Acts of "Love"

Culture has redefined love with the help of the enemy. So, the love that will be discussed here is not the love of Yahweh, but the love of men and women apart from Yahweh. The enemy and those who are deceived call good evil and evil good. Woe to them (Isaiah 5:20; Proverbs 17:15; 2 Timothy 3:1-9)!!! They go as far as to call the love of Yahweh hatred and hatred the love of Yahweh. The love of Yahweh protects the whole person in the present, the God (Yahweh) willing future and eternity. The love of men and women apart from Yahweh protects a person from feeling uncomfortable emotions. Therefore, the love of men and women apart from Yahweh is about comfort and false pleasure. The enemy wants you to waive or postpone serious problems using the feelings of "love" to do it (problems in secret). This is one reason we have heard the slogan, "Do not judge me" so much in these days, even from Christians. This one reason people want to be protected from conversations and people who disagree with them. It becomes so twisted that people want to be protected from being protected. The enemy is allowed to get a grip on people when we waive or postpone serious problems. People are in danger of developing a depraved, debauched, immoral, corrupt, wicked and evil mind when we waive and postpone serious problems. People suffer in the short run and in the long run when we waive or postpone serious problems. Parents will even say that they should let the child they claim to love so much find his or her own way, preferring comfort over parenting and protection for their child. It takes courage to parent. It takes courage to seek, follow and imitate Yahweh's love in any relationship. It is better for man to hear the rebuke of the wise than to hear the song of fools (Ecclesiastes 7:5).

The enemy does not only want our love to be false love (hatred). He wants our love to be misdirected, meaning directed towards things that are not good for us to love based on Yahweh's standards. Misdirected love causes sin and suffering just like false love does. Misdirected love causes sexual sin (fornication, adultery, homosexuality, lust of the eyes). Misdirected love can cause use to be lovers of food and strong drinks (Philippians 3:19; Isaiah 5:22; Hosea 4:11; Proverbs 20:1). Misdirected love causes the sin of partiality. Partiality causes use to lose sight of those who are truly in need and show favoritism on the bases of human desire and understanding. Partiality causes us to judge outward appearances. For example, homelessness (poverty) that affects everyone is growing because we are financially partial to diversity, equity and inclusion that do not affect many at all. There is a big difference between serving others and favoritism, but misdirected love blinds us of that truth.

The Coward (II)

The enemy does not only want you to be a coward in your state of mind, but he also wants you to be a coward in the work of your hands (i.e., what you do). The main reason he desires this for us is because "…the cowardly…will be in the lake that burns with fire, which is the second death (Revelation 21:8). God tells us through the Book of James, "Be doers of the word, and not hearers only. Otherwise, you are deceiving yourselves" (James 1:22). Being cowardly will interfere with our fruit of self-control. Self-control is not just stopping ourselves from saying something or doing something when we get discernment to do so. Self-control is also engaging situations and people by saying something and/or doing something when we get discernment to do so.

IDOLATRY (OTHER LORDS)

CHAPTER IV

One of Those Types of Christians

The enemy wants you to have moderation in our religion. Sometimes this moderation in our religion causes us and others to feel like we fit in with the world. It causes us to look more like the world. People will see us no different than they see a nonbeliever, a heathen, a pagan. The enemy loves this because he does not want you to be one of those devoted Christians. He does not want you to be one of the Christians who is always involving the Lord in your mind set and behavior. That is understandable because if we have moderation in our religion, it makes room for us to have other lords. It makes room for us to worship and rely on worldly things. It makes room for our faith to shrink back. This would not be pleasing to Yahweh but would be pleasing to the enemy. Yeshua gives a famous warning to the church in Ephesus due to their moderation as He says, "I know your deeds, that you are neither cold nor hot. I wish you were either one or the other! So, because you are lukewarm—neither hot nor cold—I am about to spit you out of my mouth." (Revelation 3:15-16). It is clear that Yeshua hates moderation.

There is a conventional wisdom that says, "Do everything in moderation". Well, we can see that is not good advice. One thing I like to say is, "I have dependent personality disorder because I depend on my Lord and Savior Yeshua Christ for everything". The Word of Yahweh tells us, "My son, if you receive my words and treasure up my commandments with you...if you seek it like silver and search for it as for hidden treasure, then you will understand the fear of the Lord and find the knowledge of Yahweh" (Proverbs 2:1-5). The Word of Yahweh also says, "Never let loving devotion or faithfulness leave you; bind them around your neck, write them on the tablet of your heart" (Proverbs 3:3). That does not sound like moderation. That sounds like excess. If we understand the effort it takes to seek silver and hidden treasure, we understand that the effort involves excessive engagement.

Work and Love

Sigmund Freud, the father of personality development in the field of psychology, said, "Love and work...work and love, that's all there is". How we interpret that statement depends on where our state of mind is focused. It depends on what or who sets the rules, guidelines, and standards in our lives. It depends on the level of moral reasoning in our decision we tend to operate from. That is, do we make decisions based on positive or negative consequences, based on social norms or based on our inner moral guidelines apart from consequences and social norms? It depends on what or who is Lord in our life. The enemy wants you to have other lords in your life other than Yeshua Christ. He is okay with and wants you to see Yeshua as your savior as long as you do not see Yeshua as your Lord. The truth is that Yeshua is Lord and Savior not just one or the other. If He is not both in our lives, then we do not have a true relationship with Him. Therefore, the enemy wants to get you to a place where you do not have a relationship with Yeshua at all or your relationship with Yeshua is only as your Savior and many have fallen into that state of mind and the behavior that follows. One way the enemy tries to get you to this point is that he wants you to be focused on economics and social things as if it is what makes up real life. As it relates to economics we hope for gain and as it relates to society, we hope for cooperation and sometimes admiration. These things can seem so tangible and concrete in our lives that we can falsely learn that they are the source and outcome of reality. The mechanisms that seem to influence our place in the economy and society can easily become our lord. Then we are drawn to exalt and devote ourselves to them in order to maintain worldly success or avoid failure.

One way we maintain this devotion is that we quickly or slowly began to be deceived and establish that only physical facts are real and spiritual ones are subjective. This mind set will challenge and even deny the fact of Spiritual objective truth. The enemy knows if we see the physical as real and the Spiritual as subjective, we will change the truth for a lie and began to worship created things instead of the creator (Romans 1:25). Therefore, this worship can range from earth itself (e.g., climate change, earth focused superstitions etc.) to mankind (honoring manmade standards over Yahweh's standards). As followers of Christ these economic and social mechanisms are mechanisms to be seen and used as resources but not the source. As followers of Christ, all aspects of life and moments in life are a battle and we always go to our Lord before engaging in battle to see if we should engage and if we are to engage, how. The enemy wants you to ignore the real life your Lord and Savior was, is and is to come.

Separation

Since the Garden of Eden, the enemy has been trying to get us to ignore Yahweh in hopes to separate us from Him. It was one sin that he wanted them to commit to disrupt their relationship with Yahweh and they did it. He wants sin to separate you from Yahweh even if they are a culmination of sin. One idol or many idols will please the enemy. This means he wants you to reject Yahweh. The Merriam-Webster's definition of reject is "to refuse to accept, consider, submit to or use". The enemy knows that if we submit to or if we use something other than the protection of our Creator, we are headed towards death physically and/or Spiritually. Hopefully we know and understand that nothing can separate us from the love of Yahweh that He has shown us in Yeshua Christ (Romans 8:38-39). This is because what He has done for us; He will never rescind or reverse. However, we can reject His love and choose sin. As mentioned before, there are consequences to creating a habit of rejecting Yahweh and choosing sin. The Word of God tells us, "…since they did not see fit to acknowledge God, God gave them up to a debased (corrupted) mind to do what ought not to be done. They were filled with all manner of unrighteousness, evil, covetousness, malice…" (Romans 1:28-29). If we are not given over to the sin that we have chosen which leads to more sin, we may find ourselves in a position where

Yahweh will not respond to our repentance in a restorative manner. Yahweh refused to restore King Saul and Esau when they tried to repent.

Our Comforter

The enemy wants you to think that you have something else to fall back on other than Yahweh and the care He provides. When we have moderation in our religion, start to see worldly things to be more real than Yahweh and His Word, and begin to choose something other than Yahweh's protection in our work and love, we will also start to use worldly things other than our Lord and Savior's love and protection to comfort us. We could develop a habit of having a drink of alcohol or a smoke after a hard day's work, during or after a stressful moment or just to start our day and think we would not be comforted without it and refuse or struggle to stop it. We could also worship sex, beauty, exercise, food, video games, money, television or social media as a comforter. We could name so many things that we could fall back on to deal with our stress or burdens as if the cross of Christ and the Power He gives is not enough. These things become idols in our lives and that is what the enemy wants. The Word of Yahweh says, "They are headed for destruction. Their god is their appetite, they brag about shameful things, and they think only about this life here on earth (Philippians 3:19). The Word of Yahweh also says, "Woe to those who rise early in the morning to run after their drinks, who stay up late at night till they are inflamed with wine." and "What sorrow for those who are heroes at drinking wine and boast about all the alcohol they can hold" (Isaiah 5:11-NIV and Isaiah 5:22-NLT).

The truth is, if you worship beauty, you will always feel ugly. If you worship intellect, you will end up feeling stupid. If you worship money, you will never feel like you have enough (David Wallace). If you worship food, you will always have an appetite. If you worship entertainment, you will always feel bored. If you worship drugs, including alcohol, you will always feel angst. If you worship anything other than our Creator, you will not ever be satisfied. Yeshua lets us know that He gives everlasting water (John 4:10).

THE SELF

CHAPTER V

Selfish Prayers

One of the most difficult things to do is to ignore the self. Therefore, when we pray you can imagine how often our self can interfere with or contaminate that communication. The enemy wants our prayers to be soulish (i.e., selfish) as opposed to setting aside our souls (naked souls) to get Yahweh's perspective. At the core, soulish prayers are prayers that are not aligned with the character of our Lord and Savior. They are not self-denying, humble, or lacking conceited ambition (Philippians 2:3-4). They can even be envious and therefore covetous. They can be ignorant of the needs of others. They can be unrepentant. This is what the enemy wants. Why? He knows that Yahweh will more than likely not listen to those prayers and unanswered prayers create doubt. Some believe that Yahweh listens to all prayers, but He does not. He tells us in His Word, "When you spread out your hands in prayer, I will hide My eyes from you; even though you multiply your prayers, I will not listen" (Isaiah 1:15). His

Word also tells us, "The LORD is far from the wicked, but He hears the prayer of the righteous" (Proverbs 15:29). This truth is taught to us again as He says, "...husbands must give honor to your wives. Treat your wife with understanding as you live together. She may be weaker than you are, but she is your equal partner in God's gift of new life. Treat her as you should so your prayers will not be hindered (1 Peter 3:7).

To avoid the soulish prayers that the enemy wants, we can love and gain Divine knowledge, humble ourselves and gain understanding focus and meaningfully pray the Holy Scripture that says, "Search me, God, and know my heart; test me and know my anxious thoughts. See if there is any offensive way in me, and lead me in the way everlasting (Psalm 139:23-24). As we grow in the Lord, He will urge our hearts towards His purpose, standards and His will. We become more like Him as we grow, less like our fallen selves, and less like the enemy and the world. He tells us in His Word, "...we all, who with unveiled faces contemplate the Lord's glory, are being transformed into his image with ever-increasing glory, which comes from the Lord, who is the Spirit (2 Corinthians 3:18). Therefore, when Yeshua says, "I tell you, whatever you ask in prayer, believe that you have received it, and it will be yours" (Mark 11:24) and when He says, "Ask, and it will be given to you; seek, and you will find; knock, and the door will be opened to you" (Matthew 7:7), we must understand that as we grow in Him, His desires and purpose will become our desires and purpose. This will be reflected in our prayers and our prayers will not be soulish. Yahweh loves His standards and purpose, and He responds when those He loves are in line with them in prayer.

Self-centered Self

The enemy wants to keep you focused unwaveringly on yourself rather than Yahweh. This is different than praying soulish prayers. Prayer is very important part of our relationship and religion with our Creator, but the enemy knows that there are other parts to that relationship, and he wants to destroy those as well. The other things we do to seek, know, understand, and obey Yahweh are numerous. We can gather with other believers. We can have daily reading of His Word by ourselves or with others. We can serve those in need in some way. We can choose to forgive someone. We can choose to parent our children. We can take a drive to the store. We can watch different shows on our television. We can find entertainment on our cell phones. We can choose what outfit to buy and wear. We can choose what words to use in a conversation. This list can go on and on because life is full of things we think and do.

If the enemy is successful with getting you to focus unwaveringly on yourself rather than Yahweh, you will habitually socially compare yourself to others and/or place undue value on your mental representations (e.g., your truth). When this happens, you will lose sight of a Biblical worldview. The many different things that we can choose to think or do will be subject to our instincts, social norms and our own understanding, but not subject to the Word of Yahweh. They will ultimately be misunderstood. ignored, mishandled, neglected, belittled, or foreclosed. We will find ourselves seeking happiness and not joy. We will find ourselves seeking comfort and not shalom (i.e., whole, complete and harmonious peace).

Self-centered Fear

The enemy wants you to be more concerned about what can happen to you than what you do. In our culture, we have even made it a norm to avoid talking about religion and politics. People are conforming to this norm or being conditioned to be concerned about starting or engaging religious and political conversations. However, these two topics, especially religion, are the most important things to talk about because they affect everyone in time and in eternity. Why would we avoid them even if they sometimes become uncomfortable? It is true, different things can happen to us when we live out our faith and speak Yahweh's truth in light conversations and in deep conversations. The enemy knows that self-centered fear will cause us to hesitate, respond impulsively or not respond at all. The problem with this concern about what can happen to us is that we are being disobedient and inconsiderate of others if we do not have the courage to do what the Holy Spirit leads us to do. The Word of Yahweh teaches us, "...how can they call on Him to save them unless they believe in Him? And how can they believe in Him if they have never heard about Him? And how can they hear about Him unless someone tells them?" (Romans 10:14). Peter and John in the Book of Acts did the opposite of what the enemy wanted. They were more concerned about what they were doing than what would happen to them. They were thrown in jail for what they were doing (sharing the Gospel of Yeshua Christ) but refused to stop doing it even once they were released, beaten and threatened. I love to read when Peter and John say to their jailers, "Which is right in God's eyes: to listen to you, or to Him? You be the judges! As for us, we cannot help speaking about what we have seen and heard." (Acts 4:19-20).

In the times we live in, we can run into opposition to us sharing the Gospel and hopefully we are more concerned about what we do as opposed to what can happen to us. We also have faithful activities of daily living that can run into opposition. Daniel, Joseph (Son of Jacob), John the Baptist, Nicodemus and many others in Scripture are great examples of being concerned about what we do and not what can happen to us. Daniel wanted to honor Yahweh with his diet lifestyle and prayer life in the face of opposition. Joseph wanted to honor God in how he respected marriage and authority in the face of opposition. John the Baptist wanted to warn Herod of his sexual immorality in the face of opposition. Nicodemus participated in the proper burial of Yeshua Christ, which could have and may have ruined his standing with the Pharisees. We can definitely think of times when what we put in our bodies, when and where we pray, our desire to want to pray, what we say or do in regard to marriage, what we say or do in regard to sexual immorality, doing the opposite of others in regards to another person and much more will be at odds to someone or some group. It is in these times, that the enemy also wants you to be more concerned with what can happen to you than what you do.

Unawareness

The enemy does not want you to be self-aware. If you take the time to really think about the harm that we can do to ourselves and others if and when we are not self-aware you will be certain that self-awareness is important. We can be aware of ourselves in many different ways. We have an overabundance of experiences that can help us to become aware of ourselves. We can become aware of ourselves in relation to different people, places, things, and times, when no one is looking versus when someone is looking. We can come to conclusions about ourselves in relation to the presence of specific personal characteristics and/or a global sense of self. However, the most important thing in becoming self-aware is being sure not to lean on our own understanding, but trust Yahweh's perspective about everything about us and being humble enough to submit in order to gain understanding (Proverbs 3:5-6). We can get that understanding directly from Yahweh's Word and from someone in our life who He has put there to share things with us and help us explore and think clearly with a Biblical self-view. Now hopefully you can see why the enemy wants you to be self-unaware. It takes us further from the knowledge of Yahweh. It allows us and the enemy to have more opportunities to deceive and destroy in many different areas of our lives and the lives of others. Yahweh warns us that His people perish when they lack knowledge and ignore His Spiritual Righteous Ruling (Hosea 4:6). The self-awareness we gain through relationship with Him protects us and helps us protect others, not from righteous conflicts, sufferings, and offense but from worldly and self-deception and destruction.

It's Your Time

The enemy wants you to be stingy with your time. When we are stingy with time that we devote to ourselves or time that we devote to someone else, we miss opportunities to serve others that we could serve. We may find ourselves not going beyond praying for someone when we could do more. The Book of James (2:15-16) gives us an example of this when we are asked, "If a brother or sister is poorly clothed and lacking in daily food, and one of you says to them, "Go in peace, be warmed and filled," without giving them the things needed for the body, what good is that?" Yeshua even taught that people would be left behind or redirected when they wanted to use their time for other things instead of following Him (Luke 9:59-62). Basically, being stingy with time is self-exaltation at its core. It is the posture of the enemy, and he wants us to imitate him.

One major commandment for those who are Christian or consider themselves to be Christian is to make time to meet with other Christians regularly and without ceasing (Hebrew 10:25). This Yahweh breathed Scripture also says that some have made it a habit not to meet. Being stingy with your time does not give you the opportunity to be present and encouraging to others. This type of encouragement of one another is crucial for the Body of Christ. How can we motivate one another towards acts of love and good deeds if we are stingy with our time. Yeshua loves the Church (Ephesians 5:25) and if we want to be like Him, as we follow Him, that has to be our striving as well.

Sometimes we make assumptions about our future time. If you are stingy with your time those assumptions become expectations. We will expect certain things and activities to happen. We will speak as if they are inevitable. The Word Yahweh teaches us, "Now listen, you who say, "Today or tomorrow we will go to this or that city, spend a year there, carry on business and make money." Why, you do not even know what will happen tomorrow. What is your life? You are a mist that appears for a little while and then vanishes. Instead, you ought to say, "If it is the Lord's will, we will live and do this or that." (James 4:13-15). His Word also teaches us in, "Do not boast about tomorrow, for you do not know what a day may bring." (Proverbs 27:1)

RELATIONSHIPS

CHAPTER VI

Broken Relationship with Yeshua

The enemy wants you to see Yeshua as a "historical Yeshua". Yeshua's time on earth in the flesh was a part of the history of this world. That is what makes it easier for the enemy to get us to see Yeshua as a "historical Yeshua". Also, living in a so-called modern society, historical things can sometimes be seen as antiquated, outdated, or obsolete. Many nonbelievers use this as an argument against faith in Yeshua or a reason for them not to believe. We can be certain that Yeshua is not just a "historical Yeshua" by reading what our Lord God says in Revelation 1:8, "I am the Alpha and the Omega," says the Lord God, "who is, and who was, and who is to come, the Almighty.". Yeshua is history, present, future and eternal. He is not simply historical. Things that we classify as historical seems and become distant to us. Things that are distant to us are difficult to connect with.

The enemy wants you to not connect moral teachings to the teaching of Yeshua. He is fine with you being a moral person as long as you do not connect your morality to a relationship with Yeshua. The enemy knows that morality, being a "good" person, does not save anyone. Angus Buchan (Evangelist and author from South Africa) has the habit of screaming, "Good people" do not go to "Heaven", Believers go to Heaven". We all have heard or maybe we have even said something like this ourselves, "He was a good person. I know he is in Heaven" or "She is such a good person. I know she is going to Heaven". Yeshua tells us in Mark 10:18, "...No one is good except Yahweh alone". In Isaiah 64:6 we learn, "We are all infected and impure with sin. When we display our righteous deeds, they are nothing but filthy rags...". People like Charles Darwin and Sigmund Freud lost their faith in Yeshua because they could not mentally and emotionally handle the truth that morality is not enough to save people. They could not fathom that their "good" unbelieving loved ones would end up in Hell. If we have a historical view of Yeshua only, it will be easier for us not to connect moral teachings to Him and possibly believe that morals are all we need for eternal life.

Ultimately, the enemy does not want you to have a devotional life toward Yeshua. Yes, if we see Him only as historical and/or do not connect moral teachings to Him, it can interfere with our devotion to Him. If we see Him as Savior and not Lord or

Lord and not Savior, it will interfere with our devotion to Him. In our comfortable and convenient culture, we frequently experience people having a relationship with Yeshua as Savior only. We must all make sure that we seek a devoted relationship with Him as Lord as well. The word devoted means, to give yourself over, to commit and be loyal (Merriam-Webster). The word lord means, having authority and power over others (Merriam-Webster). The word savior means, saving from danger and destruction and giving salvation. Therefore, if we put this all together our relationship with Yeshua is us giving ourselves over, committing and being loyal to Yeshua's authority and power and Yeshua's ability to save us from danger and destruction and give us salvation. Therefore, we must know and understand, to our best ability, His Authority (through Yahweh), His Power (by the Holy Spirit), His Protection and His Salvation (through His life, death, and resurrection) and not leave room for any other. We must do this because; Christ is not valued at all unless He is valued above all (Augustine). We must do this because Yahweh says, "I will not yield my glory to another". We can know and understand to our best ability by asking through prayer, reading/listening to His Scripture, and engaging the Church (i.e., His body).

Broken Relationship with the Body of Yeshua

The enemy wants to pull you away from mature Christians in your stressful times and away from certain scriptures. It makes sense that the enemy wants this because a mature Christian is one who can discern good and evil. We learn in the book Hebrews 5:14, "...solid food (i.e., Word of righteousness) is for the mature (i.e., those skilled in the Word of righteousness), who by constant use have trained themselves to distinguish good from evil". We lose connection with community and Truth that can help with positive change that makes us more like Yeshua when we are pulled away from mature Christians. We may seek Christians who are not as mature and scriptures that are less challenging and less sharpening because it seems safer. If our down time is connected to sin, we may run into the serious problem of not repenting and being healed. The Word of Yahweh tells us to "Confess your sins to each other and pray for each other so that you may be healed. The earnest prayer of a righteous person has great power and produces wonderful results." (James 5:16). The enemy wants to keep us from these wonderful results. Yahweh never leads us to do anything that is contrary to the Bible (Billy Graham). If the stressful time is not connected to sin, being pulled away can still put us in a dangerous position to be blind to things that we need to see. We may find ourselves choosing responses that are obviously wrong or responses that are wrong in a subtle way (i.e., almost right). Staying connected to our brothers and sisters in Yeshua has obvious benefits to our continued growth. Also, we create closer and deeper relationships when we connect with each other during stressful times as well as good times. We are called to, "Rejoice with those who rejoice, weep with those who weep and live in harmony with one another" (Romans 12:15-16). If we only connect with our good times, we will ultimately create mental distance that does not distinguish the support we seek based on maturity.

The enemy wants to keep you mentally distant from the Church and your true self. We naturally will not show and talk about certain things that are on our minds when we become compartmental in our interactions with the other Christians in our lives. We create a pattern of consistent high self-monitoring. High self-monitors withhold certain things that are on their minds and behave in ways that are not genuine and guarded. We will find ourselves extending this fake presentation to all Christians (i.e., the Church) we meet. This condition keeps us from truly loving one another. It is understandable that we sometimes need time to develop trust or overcome past negative experiences, but we do not want to let these things be an opportunity for the enemy to step in and cause this distance to become permanent. The Word of

Yahweh teaches us how He wants us to be with one another that does not include fake presentations. He tells us that because we are made new and created to be like Him each of us must put off falsehood and speak truthfully to our neighbor, for we are all members of one body (Ephesians 4:25). He also commands us to love one another and to let love be genuine (Romans 12:9). The potential for distance between us and the Church and distance from our true self can even cause pessimistic instability in finding a church home.

The enemy wants you to church hop as critics. We are likely to change church congregations when we do not develop mature and genuine relationships. However, we will more than likely never see the lack of those types of relationships as the cause of our changing churches. Therefore, we will attribute the church hop to something that has nothing to do with us personally but more external. We will find something wrong within each church congregation as a reason to hop to another congregation. We stay blind to the fact that it is the lack of being mindful of ourselves and the lack of mature and genuine relationships that is the true issue we face. It is understandable that sometimes we run into false churches. The enemy wants pastors to water down Christianity and to be narrow and limited in the truth they preach about. He wants the pastor to fear losing members or to be so deceived or self-serving that the truth is far from him. However, this type of church hopping is not because of the existence of that evil. The enemy would love for you to end up at a false church. The type of church hopping that occurs after experiencing a true church (not perfect, but true) is the type the enemy wants, and he wants us to be critics of those true churches. Ultimately, he wants you to never find a Christian community, which is the body of Yeshua, to do life and grow with.

Wicked Blood

The enemy wants you to get caught up in traditions regarding blood relatives instead of Yahweh's truth just like we see the Pharisees (religious leaders) do with different traditions in the Gospels. He wants culture to create a norm and tradition that blood relatives are the closest relationships we should have. He wants you to conform to this tradition and believe that you must be in relationship with blood relatives. This does not just pertain to you but even your children if you have them. Therefore, he wants you to develop a strong obligation to give blood relatives access to your life and your children's lives if you have them. The enemy wants you to feel this obligation and be yoked to the blood relative(s) if the blood relative is a believer or not. He wants us to see our blood relatives as our true family, especially if they are not believers in Yeshua or if they are lukewarm disobedient so-called Christians. The enemy then wants you to exalt and become prideful about your blood relative group. It might be hard to believe but it is a cultural tradition to believe that blood relatives are our true family, and our Lord and Savior was clear about that in His word and His actions. First with the words He spoke, we learn from our Lord and Savior Himself who our true family is. Yeshua publicly announced in Matthew 12:50 that His family is whoever does the will of Yahweh. Therefore, He does not consider those who do not do the will of Yahweh to be His family. He is teaching us that His true family and our true family are those who are obedient and seek obedience. The enemy does not want you to see only those who are obedient as family. He wants you to see those who are disobedient as your family. The enemy wants you to put your blood relatives' desires and lifestyles before the love and teachings of Christ as your Lord. Our Lord warns us that, "Anyone who loves their father or mother more than me is not worthy of me; anyone who loves their son or daughter more than me is not worthy of me". (Matthew 10:37). Yeshua gives an even more stern warning when he said, "If you want to be my disciple, you must, by comparison, hate everyone else - your father and mother, wife and children, brothers, and sisters – yes even their own life. Otherwise, you cannot be my disciple". (Luke 14:26). Yeshua knew that our exaltation of family could cause us to choose them over Him which would destroy us. It would destroy us because we would be ignoring the greatest commandment to 'Love the Lord your God with all your heart and with all your soul and with all your mind.' (Matthew 22:37). The enemy longs for our destruction. He wants our faith and obedience to become contaminated, to shrink and become secondary to our loyalty to blood relatives who are not our true family, eternal family. Before Yeshua gives us these warnings, in the book of Matthew and Luke, we find Him, in Matthew 10:35-36, sharing, "I have come to set a man against his father, a daughter against her mother, and a daughter-in-law against her mother-in-law. Your enemies will be right in your own household". Why does He proclaim this? We see why in Luke 12:52 when He says, "From now on families will be split apart, three in favor of me, and two against or two in favor and three against". It has to do with favor in Him over all else. The enemy does not want this split between you and your blood relatives due your favor in Yeshua. He wants your approval of or excessive tolerance of disobedience that causes you to participate in sin or overlook it. The enemy wants you and your children to be torn between what pleases Yahweh and what blood relatives do. This will ensure the disruption or turn from growth in the Lord for us. The enemy hopes it will make parenting difficult as well, as the child aligns with blood relatives who are disobedient. He wants to make it difficult for us to change in the right direction if that direction is away from what blood relatives do or think in their lives. I have seen too many times someone not be able to change and grow in their faith walk because the blood relative group has not changed. They would have to view their blood relative group differently if they were to change and that was just too hard for them. They loved the blood relative(s) more than they loved Yahweh.

Secondly, in His actions Yeshua showed who He believed to be family. I think we all know that Mary, Yeshua's mother, had other children after she gave birth to Yeshua. She had other sons. However, right before His death, Yeshua left His mother in the care of John and told Mary that John was now her son and He told John that Mary was now his mother and Mary went to live with John (John 19:25-27). Why did Yeshua do this? Mary had other blood relatives (sons) she could have lived with. He could have just let Mary return to one of her sons. Yeshua obviously saw John as family due to his obedience and the blood relatives as not family due to their disobedience that was born out of their unbelief. The enemy loves the saying, "Blood is thicker than water". However, it is not thicker than the Living Water (i.e., Holy Spirit) that comes from our relationship with Yeshua Christ as Lord and Savior. St Paul tells us in 2 Corinthians 5:16 that he no longer regarded anyone according to the flesh, a worldly point of view. The enemy does not want us to do the same.

Wicked Love

Studies show that 98% of unmarried people in the United States want to be married. Also, in this culture, love is the main reason people say they get married. This can be a problem for many because the enemy wants you to see marriage as only being in love. So, if we as Christians see marital love as being in love only or mostly, we are in trouble. The problem with seeing marital love as being in love only or mostly is that being in love is usually attached to emotions related to euphoria. The enemy wants you to operate in enchantment instead of true love in marriage. He wants this because he wants you to be able to say to your wife (if you are a man) or your husband (if you are woman), "I have fallen out of love with you". However, he knows that it takes more than this to destroy your marriage or destroy your family, divorce or not. What the enemy wants is for you to also have a distorted expectation and perception of marriage. He wants you to see being in love as more important than loyalty, mutual help, preservation of charity and transmission of life. The end goal he has is for you to see sexual infatuation as love if marriage is intended to happen and if marriage is intended to persist. So, if those companionate and commitment factors in marriage are healthy but they do not create jubilance frequent enough or sexual infatuation decreases, the marriage will still struggle or end. However, distorted expectations and perceptions are not always directly related to the feeling of being in love and sexual infatuation. The enemy will try to get us to expect our spouses to be totally responsible for maintaining our happiness. He will try to get us to expect our spouses to be able to read our minds about something we desire or dislike. He will want us to expect our spouses to have romantic characteristics that we liked in another romantic relationship. He wants us to expect marriage to have no crisis. He wants us to expect nothing but togetherness (no autonomy) or too much autonomy. He wants us to perceive marriage as a contract that can be broken not a covenant that is truly until death even if we give that oath in a marital ceremony.

Wicked Marriage

The enemy wants you to marry someone who thinks the Christian life is intensely difficult. This state of mind about the difficulty of the Christian life is brought about by the same deception that was used in the Garden of Eden to deceive Eve. Satan, at that time, rephrased what Yahweh actually said and purposely ignored the wonderful Yahweh given provision that was given to Adam and Eve. He interjected a pessimistic view about one mind set and behavior that led to gracious provision and eternal life and he interjected an optimistic motivation to think and do the opposite that led to death. If he can get you to marry someone who will do the same towards a Christian life, he can begin to work his pessimistic deception through them. For it to be easier to get us to this point, he wants to guide us away from equally yoked marriages. The Word of Yahweh commands and teaches us, "Do not be unequally yoked with unbelievers. For what partnership has righteousness with lawlessness? Or what fellowship has light with darkness?" (2 Corinthians 6:14). It is easier for him to influence unequally yoked marriages if we already have a state of mind that being in love (jubilation) and/or sexual infatuation, as aforementioned, is the grand necessity for marriage combined with a tunnel vision state of mind that these grand necessities are actually "irresistible love", which we discussed in chapter 3. These so-called "love grand necessities" will cause us to overlook, at least initially, the differences someone has in morals, values and attitudes towards very important things in our lives or even worse, cause us to think that these differences will not interfere with anything in our marriage.

Relational Deficit

Life is basically full of relational experiences. There are basically two ways we can exist in relationships. We can be cooperative, or we can be aggressive. Cooperation is when two or more people interact in a mutual benefiting way. This takes different levels of effort, depending on the type of relationship combined with the type of situation combined with a person's personal characteristics. Therefore, cooperation can be easy or difficult, simple or complex. The spoken or unspoken objective of sane individuals is to create helpful and healthy interactions. This has nothing to do with emotions but the reality and morality of the interaction that leads to living in and living out what is objectively true and therefore beneficial for the moment and for the long run. Of course, these cooperative interactions have ebbs and flows, ups and downs, but the ups outweigh and are more frequent than the downs and the ebbs and flows are more of a challenge than a threat to the relationship. Of course, this takes honesty, maturity and observation of self, others, and situations. Aggression is the opposite of cooperation. Aggression is not used for mutual benefit.

Aggression is harmful. Most people think of physical aggression when they hear the word "aggression". However, there are different types of aggression. There is physical, relational, verbal, reactive, instrumental aggression, and others. Each type of aggression can be intended or unintended to be harmful. We must keep in mind that cooperation can seem aggressive, and aggression can seem cooperative. This is because cooperation can sometimes seem harsh (e.g., constructive criticism) and aggression can sometimes seem kind (e.g., blind affirmation). Constructive criticism is beneficial and therefore cooperation. Blind affirmation is harmful and therefore aggression. Proverbs 27:6 teaches us, "Wounds from a sincere friend are better than many kisses from an enemy". A similar wisdom is shared in Proverbs 28:23 as it says, "In the end, people appreciate honest criticism far more than flattery". It takes honesty, maturity and observation of self, others, and situations to successfully control our aggression. If we interact well with others in these simple and/or complex situations, we have high interpersonal ability. If we do not interact well, we have low interpersonal ability.

The enemy wants to confuse and distress your relationships; therefore, he does not want you to have interpersonal awareness while being self-unaware at the same time. Basically, he wants you to be unaware of others and unaware of yourself when you have interactions. This unawareness of others can even include our Lord and Savior. We discussed self-unawareness in "The Self" chapter and hopefully we understand how our self-unawareness can be harmful to others and that Yahweh's statutes and instructions are the best source for us to gain self-awareness (i.e., knowledge and understanding of self). It is difficult to for us to change something of which we are unaware and if it does change, we would not be aware of what changed. The same goes for interpersonal unawareness. It causes harm, it is unproductive, and we can gain more interpersonal awareness through the statutes and instructions of Yahweh. If the enemy does not get what he wants we will be deeply aware of ourselves, deeply aware of others, especially in close relationships, and be able to discern the different effective and ineffective ways to respond to people as we interact with them. If the enemy gets what he wants, we will not have this awareness and we will interact with people in ineffective, inconsiderate, and even deceptive and destructive ways. We will find ourselves longing for shalom in a relationship but perplexed on how to accomplish it.

As you struggle to get close relationships back on track the enemy wants you to be double minded in your relationships. That is, he wants you to participate in false approval of behaviors and mind sets while you maintain your vanity (i.e., egotism).

In false approval he wants you to be silent when you ought to speak and laugh when you ought to be silent (C.S. Lewis). That silence and laughter comes off as cooperative but can be actually aggressive if it is harmful. In vanity, he wants you to be aware of the false approval in your private times, away from that person, and hopefully compare that disapproval to others in your life that you approve of. At this point, you will be double-minded in your specific (i.e., microcosm) interactions and double-minded wholly (i.e., macrocosm) in your interactions. The enemy wants this double-minded position you are in to frustrate you and for you to see the person to whom you offer false approval to as the source of your frustration. He wants you to continue to waiver on your own opinion about the false approval and develop grudges after doing so. This drives you deeper into a dysfunctional relationship and keeps you from being honest due to grudges seeming like mountains instead of mole hills. False approval (i.e., wavering on the truth) turns into grudges. Grudges drain us and are not pleasing to Yahweh. However, the enemy wants fatigue to cause resentment in our relationships. He has now gotten us to a position of being dishonest, suffering and unforgiveness. The Word of Yahweh warns us to, "See to it that no one falls short of the grace of God and that no bitter root grows up to cause trouble and defile many." (Hebrews 12:15). Honest engagement may seem difficult sometimes and may even end relationships on certain levels, but it will never end or challenge our relationship with Yahweh or our shalom.

Impulsive Gratification

As Christians we work out our salvation in relation to our faith in our Lord God. We seek to have fruit that is like His fruit. So, we will embrace certain things and reject others, rightfully so. However, the enemy still wants to be deceptive enough to turn these desires against us and others. As we develop ways of life that are in line with our faith, we can become legalistic or impulsive and seek immediacy from others. The enemy wants your sense of avoiding some behaviors (e.g., profanity, gluttony, greed, honesty, sexual immorality etc.) to be insensitive to others' presence, efforts, and time. C.S. Lewis tells a story about a Christian who has internalized moral decisions about their diet lifestyle and while at a restaurant the waiter makes a mistake with their order causing the Christian to become rude and insensitive to the waiter out of frustration to maintain their sense of loyalty related to their diet lifestyle. This Christian had developed a diet lifestyle to avoid what they considered to be gluttony. So, the enemy hopes that in their desire to not be gluttonous, they become gluttonous (i.e., excessive) about avoiding gluttony (i.e., excessiveness). This is the same pattern he is looking for with every Yahweh desire we have. It may look a little different, but he wants to twist it so that you become aggressive, especially towards those who actually have a soft heart towards Yeshua but maybe has not made a firm decision about following Him. A general way to look at how a Christian can end up responding is impatience. It is difficult living in a body and world of fallenness and we love and sometimes long to see Yahweh's righteous. This love and longing can easily become the need for impulsive gratification which can in turn create unnecessary relationship problems. Proverbs 14:29 teaches us, "Whoever is slow to anger has great understanding, but he who has a hasty temper exalts folly".

Immediate Gratification

As we live in this world, we all develop likes and dislikes. We also develop habits and pet peeves. These habits and pet peeves become delicacies. The enemy wants your delicacies to be dysfunctional in human relations. Most of the time these delicacies are common and not connected to good or evil but can be in the context of moments that could become good or evil. We might have delicacies related to where we sit at church, how people use merge lanes, getting coffee in the morning. how someone addresses us, what we do and don't do on certain days, what time we go to bed, what time we get up, what we like to drink with certain foods; hopefully you get the picture. If we do not get or we are denied our delicacies, we can become irritable. The enemy wants you to indulge to the point you feel put out if you cannot have your indulged thing. The Word of Yahweh warns us, "You desire but do not have, so you kill. You covet but you cannot get what you want, so you quarrel and fight. You do not have because you do not ask God." (James 4:2). This truth can be applied to so many different things on so many different levels. The enemy wants us to kill, covet, quarrel and fight and hopefully we are self-aware through Yahweh enough to instead produce love, joy, peace, patience, kindness, goodness, faithfulness, gentleness, and self-control (Galatians 5:22-23), not how the world define these things but how Yahweh does.

JOY STEALER IN SUFFERINGS

CHAPTER VII

Bittersweet

Conformity is a powerful thing. The reasons we conform are powerful as well. Conformity is doing or thinking something simply because others are doing it or thinking it. It is considered implied pressure. We see others doing or thinking something and so it is implied that they would want us to do it or think it as well. There has not been a request or demand to do the behavior or have the thought when someone conforms. Conformity usually relieves feelings of angst. Therefore, it can be bittersweet. We might think something is wrong, but we conform anyway to avoid conflict. A study was conducted by Solomon Ash (1951) and has been replicated several times over the decades that showed people will conform to something they know is wrong 65% to 75% of the time to avoid feeling and being different. This outcome was alarming in 1951 and is still alarming today. Gloria Gather once said, "There may be no trumpet sound or loud applause when we make the right decision, just a calm sense of resolution and peace". Hopefully as Christ followers we choose the inner peace and calm that comes with doing what is right over the perceived outward acceptance that comes with conformity.

We might consider or start conforming to a behavior or thought and end up liking that behavior or thought regardless if others are doing it or not. If that happens, it is no longer conformity. The enemy hates this if it leads to us liking something that Yahweh commands. He does not want us conforming to Yahweh's ways but if we do, he does not want us to end up liking them. The enemy loves it when we end up liking behaviors or thoughts that are disobedient. Of course, he wants more than that. The enemy wants us to conform to worldly things above the things we really like. In this position, he does not want us to end up liking worldly behaviors and thoughts that we have conformed to because he does not just want us to be disobedient but to steal our joy as well. Conforming to disobedience (i.e., evil) and not liking it is not joyful. We are taught, "Do not be conformed to this world, but be transformed by the renewal of your mind, that by testing you may discern what is the will of God, what is good and acceptable and perfect." (Romans 12:2). Through obedience or conformity to good, acceptable, and perfect things in faith we find the true sweetness of joy.

Long Suffering

The enemy wants to keep you long suffering. This should be no surprise. However, he does not want our suffering to cause us to lean on Yeshua for the rest that is promised to us by Him, through Him, and in Him (Matthew 11:28). Yeshua understands suffering because He suffered. Yeshua's suffering did not only take place on the cross. That is what many people think about when His suffering is mentioned. Yes, Yeshua suffered for us on the cross. Thank You, thank You, thank You Yeshua! However, His suffering for us started long before the cross. Yeshua also suffered for us His entire life as He was fully human and did not sin. It requires suffering to overcome sin and the world while being human. We understand in our lives how hard it is to not have that drink, to not give in to that lust, to not gossip about that person, to not use profanity in a stressful situation, to not watch certain things that are not wholesome, to not be around certain people who are not good for us, to miss a certain thing we enjoy to help someone in need, to not participate in sex before marriage, and so on. We could add much more to this list. As we read the Gospels and pay close attention, we will see that Yeshua suffered physically, mentally, relationally, financially (with much and with little) during His time here. Yeshua overcame all His suffering. This is one reason He says, towards the end of His time in this world, that in Him we can have peace and He has overcome the world (John 16:33). Suffering in this life can happen in many different ways and there is an added uniqueness for the followers of Yeshua. Our sufferings can come from the many different spiritual, physical, mental, financial and relational challenges and threats in this world but hopefully we see our suffering that comes from obedience makes us more like Yeshua. The Word of Yahweh teaches us, "For just as we share abundantly in the sufferings of Christ, so also our comfort abounds through Christ." (2 Corinthians 1:5). The enemy knows this, but he still wants us to find suffering that we do not connect to the suffering, peace and rest of Yeshua. First, he must influence us to see suffering like the world sees suffering. Then, he aims for us to perceive our suffering as compounded suffering with no end in sight.

The enemy wants you to think your down times will never go away. Down times in our lives usually consist of more than one unpleasant thing (i.e., more than one suffering). If these down times are repetitive and frequent enough, we can be made to believe that they will never go away. If we think something will never go away our nervous system responds as if we are experiencing a threat even if it is not a threat[1]. Therefore, we are overreacting in our thoughts and in our biological self. Also, we are being only future focused when we think that our down times will never go away. A wise person once said, that Yahweh will always deliver us when it comes to suffering and He will do it in one of three ways; 1) He will deliver us FROM suffering, meaning He will keep us from experiencing it, 2) He will deliver us THROUGH suffering, meaning He will allow us to experience it but survive it (e.g., Job) or 3) He will deliver us BY suffering, meaning He will allow us to experience it and we will not survive it in time but He will free us from it in eternity. Suffering is always perceived differently if we have eternity in mind. Yeshua tells his disciples, "Whoever wants to be my disciple must deny themselves and take up their cross and follow me. For whoever wants to save their life will lose it, but whoever loses their life for me will find it." (Matthew 16:24-25). This does not mean that we cannot ask our Father in Heaven (Yahweh) to deliver us "from" suffering that we have not experienced. Yeshua teaches us in the prayer He taught His disciples how to ask for that when He said, "… Lead us not into temptation and deliver us from evil..." (Matthew 6:13). St. Paul's experiences shows how Yahweh delivers "through" suffering as we read 2 Corinthians 6:4-10,

> "…We patiently endure troubles and hardships and calamities of every kind. We have been beaten, been put in prison, faced angry mobs, worked to exhaustion, endured sleepless nights,

and gone without food... We are ignored, even though we are well known. We live close to death, but we are still alive. We have been beaten, but we have not been killed. Our hearts ache, but we always have joy. We are poor, but we give spiritual riches to others. We own nothing, and yet we have everything."

However, if we are only past, present and/or future focused it will steal our joy and increase our sufferings. The enemy hopes that he has a lot of time to get us into a position to create a perception of never ending down times. Furthermore, he wants to use much of this time to create false perceptions and memories.

The enemy wants you to live long enough to fall away. He hopes your worldly prosperity and/or memories of failures will make this an easy task. It goes back to us being in the world but not of the world when it comes to prosperity. We must want ourselves to be in the world more so than the world being in us. However, enemy wants your established prosperity to cause you to feel that you are bonded to the world even if you are not. If you are a Christian that feel bonded to the world through your prosperity you can suffer from hatred as Yeshua tells us, "No one can serve two masters: Either he will hate the one and love the other, or he will be devoted to the one and despise the other. You cannot serve both God and money." (Matthew 6:24). The enemy knows this and wants this for each of us. However, Yeshua does not tell us not to be prosperous because Yahweh's authority and power can still save a prosperous Yeshua follower (Matthew 19:24-26). Yeshua also tells us, "And I tell you, make friends for yourselves by means of unrighteous wealth, so that when it fails, they may receive you into the eternal dwellings. One who is faithful in a very little is also faithful in much, and one who is dishonest in a very little is also dishonest in much. If then you have not been faithful in the unrighteous wealth, who will entrust to you the true riches?" (Luke 16:9-11). Therefore, the goal is to be faithful with unrighteous wealth to avoid trying to worship two masters.

As for memories of failure that tends to come with long life, the enemy hopes to have these memories contribute to suffering that leads to falling away. He hopes to distort your memories of your failures and hopes you believe that you are not forgivable. He wants you to be preoccupied with exaggerated failure. It is not that our failures were not harmful and disobedient but any failure other than blasphemy of the Holy Spirit (i.e., ongoing rejection of the work of the Holy Spirit and ascribing His work to the work of the enemy) that is identified as unforgivable is exaggerated. The enemy wants you to create this illusion about your past failures. He wants you to feel shame that aggravates and leads to despair. We do not think that we are useful and that others can be useful when we feel despair. We do not offer wisdom to others in later life when we feel despair. Hopefully St. Paul motivates us when he says, "Brothers and sisters, I do not consider myself yet to have taken hold of it [resurrection]. But one thing I do: Forgetting what is behind and straining toward what is ahead, I press on toward the goal to win the prize for which God has called me heavenward in Christ Jesus." (Philippians 3:13-14). Yeshua gives an even stronger message in Luke 9:62, "No one who puts his hand to the plow and then looks back is fit for the kingdom of God." The enemy wants us to look back and fall away. It is better to look forward with gratitude and hope. It is only with gratitude that life becomes rich (Dietrich Bonhoeffer).

Hope Deferred

The enemy wants to turn your sense of disappointment into a sense of injury. The Word of Yahweh instructs us to "Rejoice always, pray continually, give thanks in all circumstances; for this is God's will for you in Christ Jesus." (1 Thessalonians 16-18). A harder instruction is this,

"When times are good, be happy; but when times are bad, consider this: God has made the one as well as the other. Therefore, no one can discover anything about their future." (Ecclesiastes 7:14). John McAuthor says, "A thankful heart is one of the primary identifying characteristics of a believer". The pathway to the presence of Yahweh is opened through the door of thankfulness (Pastor Allen Jackson). However, if the enemy can get us to have strong expectations, he has us in a dangerous place of disappointment oppose to thankfulness. Expectation can give birth to "I deserve". We can see this being played out today in our culture. Whenever men believe they deserve something they are soon to think they have a human right to that something that they truly do not (C.S. Lewis). If we do not get what we think we deserve and have a right to, we feel, believe and act like we have been injured. An ongoing sense of injury leads to victimhood. Where there is a victim there is a perpetrator. Where there is a perpetrator there is someone to blame and hate. It is improbable that a false sense of human right can ever be satisfied which creates recurring injury with deferred hope. This is a suffering the enemy celebrates.

The enemy wants us to experience exhaustion in our suffering. Therefore, he prefers that you be moderately fatigued not absolutely exhausted. We do not have the energy for expectation and hope when we are absolutely exhausted. Absolute exhaustion can give us a mental break from a stimulus that is causing the suffering. This might leave room for thoughts that will challenge the suffering and relieve it. This is why the enemy does not want absolute exhaustion. We can still find the energy to have expectations and hope when we are moderately fatigue, and it keeps us in a cycle of disappointment. We still have the energy to stay preoccupied with our efforts towards our expectation when we are moderately fatigued. The enemy knows that we will then experience unexpected demands when we are already tired (C.S. Lewis). We then lightly torture ourselves and place stressful demands on others as we hope. Hope then changes to false hope especially if the hope is connected to an illusion of expectation or sense of "I deserve". The enemy wants you to have false hope that never comes to pass and for you not to be committed to endure. At this point, we would be stuck in a lie regarding to our hope and a sense of self-hatred because we can now sense a part of ourselves that is not committed to something we believe should be important to us. It is all deception to destroy Yahweh's most precious creation.

CONCLUSION

I must echo St. Paul when he said, "...I am afraid that just as Eve was deceived by the serpent's cunning, your minds may somehow be led astray from your sincere and pure devotion to Christ." (2 Corinthians 11:3). He goes on to say to us in 1 Corinthians 10:18-21, "I do not want you to be participants with demons. You cannot drink the cup of the Lord and the cup of demons. You cannot partake in the table of the Lord and the table of demons". There are so many ways that we can be deceived and destroyed by the enemy. We touched on different things that can happen in isolation, simultaneously and consecutively. They can happen to us, and they can happen to our brothers and sisters in Christ. I hope that the things that were discussed will give us motivation, not unGodly fear, to always be alert and understand that when we become children of Yahweh, we become drafted soldiers and warriors in Yeshua's army. Our battles are never ceasing; minor or major. This is inevitable if we are truly God's children and followers of Yeshua Christ. Revelation 12:9 & 17 teaches us that the enemy wages war against those who keep Yahweh's commands and those who hold to their testimony of Yeshua, and he leads the world astray.

This is also why we are told to put on the full armor of God so we can take a stand against the devil's schemes (Ephesians 6:11). We most also understand that we are in the enemy's territory every second of every day. We learn that this is his territory in Revelation 13:7 as it says that the enemy was given authority over every tribe, people, language and nation. However, and thankfully, we are not citizens of his demonic kingdom. And Scripture tells us that "No one serving as a soldier [of Christ Yeshua] gets entangled in civilian affairs, but rather tries to please his commanding officer" (2 Timothy 2:4). It is our commanding officer [Christ Yeshua] who is in us, and we are in Him. The One [Christ Yeshua] who is in us is greater than the one who is in the world (1 John 4:4). This is wonderful news after seeing the position we find ourselves in. Let us embrace the gift given to us to overcome. Romans 8:31 tells the truth as it says, "…If Yahweh is with us who can be against us.". Yeshua preserves all who love Him, but all the wicked He will destroy (Psalm 145:20). Therefore, we must be honest with ourselves about our love for Yeshua. The second message in Psalm 145:20 reminds me of something Oswald Chamber said, "Sin must be destroyed, not just corrected'. Let us not lose sight of our devotion to Yeshua as Savior and as Lord. In this we have an advocate before the Father—Yeshua Christ, the Righteous One (1 John 2:1). Life trials are not easy. But in Yahweh's will, each has a purpose. Often, He uses them to enlarge you (Warren Wiersbe). Eric Metaxas says, being a Christian is less about cautiously avoiding sin than about courageously and actively doing Yahweh's will. His will, not our will, be done!

Referenced Scripture

Introduction

Revelation 12:17 and 13:7 (NIV)

Then the dragon was enraged at the woman and went off to wage war against the rest of her offspring—those who keep God's commands and hold fast their testimony about Jesus.

It was given power to wage war against God's holy people and to conquer them. And it was given authority over every tribe, people, language and nation.

John 10:10 (ESV)

The thief comes only to steal and kill and destroy. I came that they may have life and have it abundantly.

John 1:12 (NIV)

Yet to all who did receive him, to those who believed in his name, he gave the right to become children of God—

Psalm 22 and 23 (ESV)

My God, my God, why have you forsaken me? Why are you so far from saving me, from the words of my groaning? My God, I cry by day, but you do not answer, and by night, but I find no rest. Yet you are holy, enthroned on the praises of Israel. In you our fathers trusted; they trusted, and you delivered them. To you they cried and were rescued; in you they trusted and were not put to shame. But I am a worm and not a man, scorned by mankind and despised by the people. All who see me mock me; they make mouths at me; they wag their heads; "He trusts in the LORD; let him deliver him; let him rescue him, for he delights in him!" Yet you are he who took me from the womb; you made me trust you at my mother's breasts. On you was I cast from my birth, and from my mother's womb you have been my God. Be not far from me, for trouble is near, and there is none to help. Many bulls encompass me; strong bulls of Bashan surround me; they open wide their mouths at me, like a ravening and roaring lion. I am poured out like water, and all my bones are out of joint; my heart is like wax; it is melted within my breast; my strength is dried up like a potsherd, and my tongue sticks to my jaws; you lay me in the dust of death. For dogs encompass me; a company of evildoers encircles me; they have pierced my hands and feet—I can count all my bones— they stare and gloat over me; they divide my garments among them, and for my clothing they cast lots. But you, O LORD, do not be far off! O you my help, come quickly to my aid! Deliver my soul from the sword, my precious life from the power of the dog! Save me from the mouth of the lion! You have rescued me from the horns of the wild oxen! I will tell of your name to my brothers; in the midst of the congregation I will praise you: You who fear the LORD, praise him! All you offspring of Jacob, glorify him, and stand in awe of him, all you offspring of Israel! For he has not despised or abhorred the affliction of the afflicted, and he has not hidden his face from him, but has heard, when he cried to him. From you comes my praise in the great congregation; my vows I will perform before those who fear him. The afflicted shall eat and be satisfied; those who seek him shall praise the LORD! May your hearts live forever! All the ends of the earth shall remember and turn to the LORD, and all the families of the nations shall worship before you. For kingship belongs to the LORD, and he rules over the nations. All the prosperous of the earth eat and worship; before him shall bow all who go down to the dust, even the one who could not keep himself alive. Posterity shall serve him; it shall be told of the Lord to the coming generation; they shall come and proclaim his righteousness to a people yet unborn, that he has done it.

The LORD is my shepherd; I shall not want. He makes me lie down in green pastures. He leads me beside still waters. He restores my soul. He leads me in paths of righteousness for his name's sake. Even though I walk through the valley of the shadow of death, I will fear no evil, for you are with me; your rod and your staff, they comfort me. You prepare a table before me in the presence of my enemies; you anoint my head with oil; my cup overflows. Surely goodness and mercy shall follow me all the days of my life, and I shall dwell in the house of the LORD forever.

John 16:8-14 (ESV)

And when he comes, he will convict the world concerning sin and righteousness and judgment: concerning sin, because they do not believe in me; concerning righteousness, because I go to the Father, and you will see me no longer; concerning judgment, because the ruler of this world is judged. "I still have many things to say to you, but you cannot bear them now. [13] When the Spirit of truth comes, he will guide you into all the truth, for he will not speak on his own authority, but whatever he hears he will speak, and he will declare to you the things that are to come. He will glorify me, for he will take what is mine and declare it to you.

Referenced Scripture

Chapter I – The Enemy

Ephesians 6:12 (NIV)

For our struggle is not against flesh and blood, but against the rulers, against the authorities, against the powers of this dark world and against the spiritual forces of evil in the heavenly realms.

Matthew 7:13 (NIV)

"Enter through the narrow gate. For wide is the gate and broad is the road that leads to destruction, and many enter through it.

Colossians 2:8 (ESV)

See to it that no one takes you captive by philosophy and empty deceit, according to human tradition, according to the elemental spirits of the world, and not according to Christ.

1 Peter 5:8 (NIV)

Be alert and of sober mind. Your enemy the devil prowls around like a roaring lion looking for someone to devour.

Romans 12:2 (ESV)

Do not be conformed to this world, but be transformed by the renewal of your mind, that by testing you may discern what is the will of God, what is good and acceptable and perfect.

1 Thessalonians 5:11 (ESV)

Therefore encourage one another and build one another up, just as you are doing.

Proverbs 3:5-6 (ESV)

Trust in the LORD with all your heart, and do not lean on your own understanding. In all your ways acknowledge him, and he will make straight your paths.

John 14:6 (ESV)

Jesus said to him, "I am the way, and the truth, and the life. No one comes to the Father except through me.

2 Corinthians 10:5 (ESV)

We destroy arguments and every lofty opinion raised against the knowledge of God, and take every thought captive to obey Christ,

Isaiah 55:8-9 (ESV)

For my thoughts are not your thoughts, neither are your ways my ways, declares the LORD.

Hebrews 5:14 (ESV)

But solid food is for the mature, for those who have their powers of discernment trained by constant practice to distinguish good from evil.

Ecclesiastes 2:1 (NIV)

I said to myself, "Come now, I will test you with pleasure to find out what is good." But that also proved to be meaningless.

Ecclesiastes 12:13-14 (NIV)

Now all has been heard; here is the conclusion of the matter: Fear God and keep his commandments, for this is the duty of all mankind. For God will bring every deed into judgment, including every hidden thing, whether it is good or evil.

Proverbs 4:23 (NIV)

Above all else, guard your heart, for everything you do flows from it.

Romans 12:2 (NIV)

Do not conform to the pattern of this world, but be transformed by the renewing of your mind…

Romans 8:14 (NIV)

For those who are led by the Spirit of God are the children of God.

Galatians 5:16 (NIV)

So I say, walk by the Spirit, and you will not gratify the desires of the flesh.

1 John 2:16 (ESV)

For all that is in the world—the desires of the flesh and the desires of the eyes and pride of life—is not from the Father but is from the world.

Isaiah 5:20 (ESV)

Woe to those who call evil good and good evil, who put darkness for light and light for darkness, who put bitter for sweet and sweet for bitter!

Referenced Scripture

Chapter II – State of Mind

Galatians 5:7-10 (NLT)

You were running the race so well. Who has held you back from following the truth? It certainly isn't God, for he is the one who called you to freedom. This false teaching is like a little yeast that spreads through the whole batch of dough! I am trusting the Lord to keep you from believing false teachings. God will judge that person, whoever he is, who has been confusing you.

1 John 2:16 (ESV)

For all that is in the world—the desires of the flesh and the desires of the eyes and pride of life—is not from the Father but is from the world.

Revelation 21:8 (NIV)

But the cowardly, the unbelieving, the vile, the murderers, the sexually immoral, those who practice magic arts, the idolaters and all liars—they will be consigned to the fiery lake of burning sulfur. This is the second death.

Proverbs 28:1 (ESV)

The wicked flee when no one pursues, but the righteous are bold as a lion.

Exodus 20:3 (ESV)

You shall have no other gods before me.

Exodus 22:16-31 (NIV)

"If a man seduces a virgin who is not pledged to be married and sleeps with her, he must pay the bride-price, and she shall be his wife. If her father absolutely refuses to give her to him, he must still pay the bride-price for virgins. "Do not allow a sorceress to live. "Anyone who has sexual relations with an animal is to be put to death. "Whoever sacrifices to any god other than the LORD must be destroyed. "Do not mistreat or oppress a foreigner, for you were foreigners in Egypt. "Do not take advantage of the widow or the fatherless. If you do and they cry out to me, I will certainly hear their cry. My anger will be aroused, and I will kill you with the sword; your wives will become widows and your children fatherless. "If you lend money to one of my people among you who is needy, do not treat it like a business deal; charge no interest. If you take your neighbor's cloak as a pledge, return it by sunset, because that cloak is the only covering your neighbor has. What else can they sleep in? When they cry out to me, I will hear, for I am compassionate. "Do not blaspheme God or curse the ruler of your people. "Do not hold back offerings from your granaries or your vats. "You must give me the firstborn of your sons. Do the same with your cattle and your sheep. Let them stay with their mothers for seven days, but give them to me on the eighth day. "You are to be my holy people. So do not eat the meat of an animal torn by wild beasts; throw it to the dogs.

Exodus 23:1-9 (NIV)

Do not spread false reports. Do not help a guilty person by being a malicious witness. "Do not follow the crowd in doing wrong. When you give testimony in a lawsuit, do not pervert justice by siding with the crowd, and do not show favoritism to a poor person in a lawsuit. "If you come across your enemy's ox or donkey wandering off, be sure to return it. If you see the donkey of someone who hates you fallen down under its load, do not leave it there; be sure you help them with it. "Do not deny justice to your poor people in their lawsuits. [7] Have nothing to do with a false charge and do not put an innocent or honest person to death, for I will not acquit the guilty. "Do not accept a bribe, for a bribe blinds those who see and twists the words of the innocent. "Do not oppress a foreigner; you yourselves know how it feels to be foreigners, because you were foreigners in Egypt.

1 John 4:1 (ESV)

Beloved, do not believe every spirit, but test the spirits to see whether they are from God, for many false prophets have gone out into the world.

Romans 1:25 (NIV)

They exchanged the truth about God for a lie, and worshiped and served created things rather than the Creator—who is forever praised. Amen.

Matthew 5:6 (NIV)

Blessed are those who hunger and thirst for righteousness, for they will be filled.

Matthew 6:24 (ESV)

No one can serve two masters, for either he will hate the one and love the other, or he will be devoted to the one and despise the other. You cannot serve God and money.

John 4:1-13 (ESV)

Now when Jesus learned that the Pharisees had heard that Jesus was making and baptizing more disciples than John (although Jesus himself did not baptize, but only his disciples), he left Judea and departed again for Galilee. And he had to pass through Samaria. So he came to a town of Samaria called Sychar, near the field that Jacob had given to his son Joseph. Jacob's well was there; so

Jesus, wearied as he was from his journey, was sitting beside the well. It was about the sixth hour. A woman from Samaria came to draw water. Jesus said to her, "Give me a drink." (For his disciples had gone away into the city to buy food.) The Samaritan woman said to him, "How is it that you, a Jew, ask for a drink from me, a woman of Samaria?" (For Jews have no dealings with Samaritans.) Jesus answered her, "If you knew the gift of God, and who it is that is saying to you, 'Give me a drink,' you would have asked him, and he would have given you living water." The woman said to him, "Sir, you have nothing to draw water with, and the well is deep. Where do you get that living water? Are you greater than our father Jacob? He gave us the well and drank from it himself, as did his sons and his livestock." Jesus said to her, "Everyone who drinks of this water will be thirsty again,

Galatians 5:22-23 (ESV)

But the fruit of the Spirit is love, joy, peace, patience, kindness, goodness, faithfulness, gentleness, self-control; against such things there is no law.

Luke 12:15-23 (ESV)

And he said to them, "Take care, and be on your guard against all covetousness, for one's life does not consist in the abundance of his possessions." And he told them a parable, saying, "The land of a rich man produced plentifully, and he thought to himself, 'What shall I do, for I have nowhere to store my crops?' And he said, 'I will do this: I will tear down my barns and build larger ones, and there I will store all my grain and my goods. And I will say to my soul, "Soul, you have ample goods laid up for many years; relax, eat, drink, be merry."' But God said to him, 'Fool! This night your soul is required of you, and the things you have prepared, whose will they be?' So is the one who lays up treasure for himself and is not rich toward God." And he said to his disciples, "Therefore I tell you, do not be anxious about your life, what you will eat, nor about your body, what you will put on. For life is more than food, and the body more than clothing.

Romans 12:3 (ESV)

For by the grace given to me I say to everyone among you not to think of himself more highly than he ought to think, but to think with sober judgment, each according to the measure of faith that God has assigned.

Joshua 1:9 (ESV)

Have I not commanded you? Be strong and courageous. Do not be frightened, and do not be dismayed, for the LORD your God is with you wherever you go."

Referenced Scripture

Chapter III – Work of the Hands

<u>Philippians 2:12-13 (ESV)</u>

Therefore, my beloved, as you have always obeyed, so now, not only as in my presence but much more in my absence, work out your own salvation with fear and trembling, for it is God who works in you, both to will and to work for his good pleasure.

<u>2 Corinthians 5:17 (ESV)</u>

Therefore, if anyone is in Christ, he is a new creation. The old has passed away; behold, the new has come.

<u>Hosea 13:14 (ESV)</u>

I shall ransom them from the power of Sheol; I shall redeem them from Death. O Death, where are your plagues? O Sheol, where is your sting? Compassion is hidden from my eyes.

<u>1 Corinthians 15:55-56 (ESV)</u>

"O death, where is your victory? O death, where is your sting?" The sting of death is sin, and the power of sin is the law.

2 Timothy 4:7 (NLT)

I have fought the good fight, I have finished the race, and I have remained faithful.

Isaiah 5:20 (ESV)

Woe to those who call evil good and good evil, who put darkness for light and light for darkness, who put bitter for sweet and sweet for bitter!

Proverbs 17:15 (ESV)

He who justifies the wicked and he who condemns the righteous are both alike an abomination to the LORD.

2 Timothy 3:1-9 (ESV)

But understand this, that in the last days there will come times of difficulty. For people will be lovers of self, lovers of money, proud, arrogant, abusive, disobedient to their parents, ungrateful, unholy, heartless, unappeasable, slanderous, without self-control, brutal, not loving good, treacherous, reckless, swollen with conceit, lovers of pleasure rather than lovers of God, having the appearance of godliness, but denying its power. Avoid such people. For among them are those who creep into households and capture weak women, burdened with sins and led astray by various passions, always learning and never able to arrive at a knowledge of the truth. Just as Jannes and Jambres opposed

Moses, so these men also oppose the truth, men corrupted in mind and disqualified regarding the faith. But they will not get very far, for their folly will be plain to all, as was that of those two men.

Ecclesiastes 7:5 (ESV)

It is better for a man to hear the rebuke of the wise than to hear the song of fools.

Philippians 3:19 ESV)

Their end is destruction, their god is their belly, and they glory in their shame, with minds set on earthly things.

Isaiah 5:22 (NIV)

Woe to those who are heroes at drinking wine and champions at mixing drinks,

Hosea 4:11 (ESV)

whoredom, wine, and new wine, which take away the understanding.

Proverbs 20:1 (ESV)

Wine is a mocker, strong drink a brawler, and whoever is led astray by it is not wise.

Revelation 21:8 (NIV)

But the cowardly, the unbelieving, the vile, the murderers, the sexually immoral, those who practice magic arts, the idolaters and all liars—they will be consigned to the fiery lake of burning sulfur. This is the second death.

<u>James 1:22 (BSB)</u>

Be doers of the word, and not hearers only. Otherwise, you are deceiving yourselves.

Referenced Scripture

Chapter IV – Idolatry (Other Lords)

Revelation 3:15-16 (NIV)

I know your deeds, that you are neither cold nor hot. I wish you were either one or the other! So, because you are lukewarm—neither hot nor cold—I am about to spit you out of my mouth.

Proverbs 2:1-5 (ESV)

My son, if you receive my words and treasure up my commandments with you, making your ear attentive to wisdom and inclining your heart to understanding; yes, if you call out for insight and raise your voice for understanding, if you seek it like silver and search for it as for hidden treasures, then you will understand the fear of the Lord and find the knowledge of God.

Proverbs 3:3 (BSB)

Never let loving devotion or faithfulness leave you; bind them around your neck, write them on the tablet of your heart.

Romans 1:25 (ESV)

because they exchanged the truth about God for a lie and worshiped and served the creature rather than the Creator, who is blessed forever! Amen.

Romans 8:38-39 (ESV)

For I am sure that neither death nor life, nor angels nor rulers, nor things present nor things to come, nor powers, nor height nor depth, nor anything else in all creation, will be able to separate us from the love of God in Christ Jesus our Lord.

Romans 1:28-29 (ESV)

And since they did not see fit to acknowledge God, God gave them up to a debased mind to do what ought not to be done. They were filled with all manner of unrighteousness, evil, covetousness, malice.

Philippians 3:19 (BSB)

They are headed for destruction. Their god is their appetite, they brag about shameful things, and they think only about this life here on earth.

Isaiah 5:11 (NIV)

Woe to those who rise early in the morning to run after their drinks, who stay up late at night till they are inflamed with wine.

<u>Isaiah 5:22 (NLT)</u>

What sorrow for those who are heroes at drinking wine and boast about all the alcohol they can hold.

<u>John 4:10 (ESV)</u>

Jesus answered her, "If you knew the gift of God, and who it is that is saying to you, 'Give me a drink,' you would have asked him, and he would have given you living water."

Referenced Scripture

Chapter V – The Self

Philippians 2:3-4 (ESV)

Do nothing from selfish ambition or conceit, but in humility count others more significant than yourselves. Let each of you look not only to his own interests, but also to the interests of others.

Isaiah 1:15 (BSB)

When you spread out your hands in prayer, I will hide My eyes from you; even though you multiply your prayers, I will not listen

Proverbs 15:29 (ESV)

The LORD is far from the wicked, but he hears the prayer of the righteous.

1 Peter 3:7 (BSB)

In the same way, you husbands must give honor to your wives. Treat your wife with understanding as you live together. She may be weaker than you are, but she is your equal partner in God's gift of new life. Treat her as you should so your prayers will not be hindered.

Psalm 139:23-24

Search me, God, and know my heart; test me and know my anxious thoughts. See if there is any offensive way in me, and lead me in the way everlasting.

2 Corinthians 3:18 (NIV)

And we all, who with unveiled faces contemplate the Lord's glory, are being transformed into his image with ever-increasing glory, which comes from the Lord, who is the Spirit.

Mark 11:24 (ESV)

Therefore I tell you, whatever you ask in prayer, believe that you have received it, and it will be yours.

Matthew 7:7 (NIV)

"Ask and it will be given to you; seek and you will find; knock and the door will be opened to you.

Romans 10:14 (NLT)

But how can they call on him to save them unless they believe in him? And how can they believe in him if they have never heard about him? And how can they hear about him unless someone tells them?

Acts 4:19-20 (NIV)

But Peter and John replied, "Which is right in God's eyes: to listen to you, or to him? You be the judges!

As for us, we cannot help speaking about what we have seen and heard."

Proverbs 3:5-6 (ESV)

Trust in the Lord with all your heart, and do not lean on your own understanding. In all your ways acknowledge him, and he will make straight your paths.

Hosea 4:6 (ESV)

My people are destroyed for lack of knowledge; because you have rejected knowledge, I reject you from being a priest to me. And since you have forgotten the law of your God, I also will forget your children.

James 2:15-16 (ESV)

If a brother or sister is poorly clothed and lacking in daily food, and one of you says to them, "Go in peace, be warmed and filled," without giving them the things needed for the body, what good is that?

Luke 9:59-62 (ESV)

To another he said, "Follow me." But he said, "Lord, let me first go and bury my father." And Jesus said to him, "Leave the dead to bury their own dead. But as for you, go and proclaim the kingdom of God." [61] Yet another said, "I will follow you, Lord, but let me first say farewell to those at my home." Jesus said to him, "No one who puts his hand to the plow and looks back is fit for the kingdom of God."

Hebrew 10:25 (ESV)

not neglecting to meet together, as is the habit of some, but encouraging one another, and all the more as you see the Day drawing near.

Ephesians 5:25 (ESV)

Husbands, love your wives, as Christ loved the church and gave himself up for her,

James 4:13-15 (ESV)

Come now, you who say, "Today or tomorrow we will go into such and such a town and spend a year there and trade and make a profit"— yet you do not know what tomorrow will bring. What is your life? For you are a mist that appears for a little time and then vanishes. Instead you ought to say, "If the Lord wills, we will live and do this or that."

Proverbs 27:1 (ESV)

Do not boast about tomorrow, for you do not know what a day may bring.

Referenced Scripture

Chapter VI – Relationships

<u>Mark 10:18 (ESV)</u>

And Jesus said to him, "Why do you call me good? No one is good except God alone.

<u>Isaiah 64:6 (NLT)</u>

We are all infected and impure with sin. When we display our righteous deeds, they are nothing but filthy rags. Like autumn leaves, we wither and fall, and our sins sweep us away like the wind.

<u>Hebrews 5:14 (NIV)</u>

But solid food is for the mature, who by constant use have trained themselves to distinguish good from evil.

<u>James 5:16 (NLT)</u>

Confess your sins to each other and pray for each other so that you may be healed. The earnest prayer of a righteous person has great power and produces wonderful results.

Romans 12:15-16 (ESV)

Rejoice with those who rejoice, weep with those who weep. Live in harmony with one another. Do not be haughty, but associate with the lowly. Never be wise in your own sight.

Ephesians 4:25 (ESV)

Therefore, having put away falsehood, let each one of you speak the truth with his neighbor, for we are members one of another.

Romans 12:9 (ESV)

Let love be genuine. Abhor what is evil; hold fast to what is good.

Matthew 12:50 (ESV)

For whoever does the will of my Father in heaven is my brother and sister and mother."

Matthew 10:37 (NIV)

Anyone who loves their father or mother more than me is not worthy of me; anyone who loves their son or daughter more than me is not worthy of me.

Luke 14:26 (NLT)

If you want to be my disciple, you must, by comparison, hate everyone else—your father and mother, wife and children, brothers and sisters—yes, even your own life. Otherwise, you cannot be my disciple.

Matthew 22:37 (ESV)

And he said to him, "You shall love the Lord your God with all your heart and with all your soul and with all your mind.

Matthew 10:35-36 (NLT)

'I have come to set a man against his father, a daughter against her mother, and a daughter-in-law against her mother-in-law. Your enemies will be right in your own household!'

Luke 12:52 (NLT)

From now on families will be split apart, three in favor of me, and two against—or two in favor and three against.

John 19:25-27 (NIV)

Near the cross of Jesus stood his mother, his mother's sister, Mary the wife of Clopas, and Mary Magdalene. When Jesus saw his mother there, and the disciple whom he loved standing nearby, he said to her, "Woman, here is your son," and to the disciple, "Here is your mother." From that time on, this disciple took her into his home.

2 Corinthians 5:16 (ESV)

From now on, therefore, we regard no one according to the flesh. Even though we once regarded Christ according to the flesh, we regard him thus no longer.

2 Corinthians 6:14 (ESV)

Do not be unequally yoked with unbelievers. For what partnership has righteousness with lawlessness? Or what fellowship has light with darkness?

Proverbs 27:6 (NLT)

Wounds from a sincere friend are better than many kisses from an enemy.

Proverbs 28:23 (NLT)

In the end, people appreciate honest criticism far more than flattery.

Hebrews 12:15 (NIV)

See to it that no one falls short of the grace of God and that no bitter root grows up to cause trouble and defile many.

Proverbs 14:29 (ESV)

Whoever is slow to anger has great understanding, but he who has a hasty temper exalts folly.

James 4:2 (NIV)

You desire but do not have, so you kill. You covet but you cannot get what you want, so you quarrel and fight. You do not have because you do not ask God.

Galatians 5:22-23 (ESV)

But the fruit of the Spirit is love, joy, peace, patience, kindness, goodness, faithfulness, gentleness, self-control; against such things there is no law.

Referenced Scripture

Chapter 7 – Joy Stealer in Sufferings

Romans 12:2 (ESV)

Do not be conformed to this world, but be transformed by the renewal of your mind, that by testing you may discern what is the will of God, what is good and acceptable and perfect.

Matthew 11:28 (ESV)

Come to me, all who labor and are heavy laden, and I will give you rest.

John 16:33 (ESV)

I have said these things to you, that in me you may have peace. In the world you will have tribulation. But take heart; I have overcome the world."

2 Corinthians 1:5 (NIV)

For just as we share abundantly in the sufferings of Christ, so also our comfort abounds through Christ.

Matthew 16:24-25 (NIV)

Then Jesus said to his disciples, "Whoever wants to be my disciple must deny themselves and take up their cross and follow me. For whoever wants to save their life will lose it, but whoever loses their life for me will find it.

Matthew 6:13 (ESV)

And lead us not into temptation, but deliver us from evil.

2 Corinthians 6:4-10 (NLT)

...We patiently endure troubles and hardships and calamities of every kind. [5] We have been beaten, been put in prison, faced angry mobs, worked to exhaustion, endured sleepless nights, and gone without food. We prove ourselves by our purity, our understanding, our patience, our kindness, by the Holy Spirit within us, and by our sincere love. We faithfully preach the truth. God's power is working in us. We use the weapons of righteousness in the right hand for attack and the left hand for defense. We serve God whether people honor us or despise us, whether they slander us or praise us. We are honest, but they call us impostors. We are ignored, even though we are well known. We live close to death, but we are still alive. We have been beaten, but we have not been killed. [10] Our hearts ache, but we always have joy. We are poor, but we give spiritual riches to others. We own nothing, and yet we have everything.

Matthew 6:24 (NIV)

No one can serve two masters. Either you will hate the one and love the other, or you will be devoted to the one and despise the other. You cannot serve both God and money.

Matthew 19:24-26 (ESV)

Again I tell you, it is easier for a camel to go through the eye of a needle than for a rich person to enter the kingdom of God." When the disciples heard this, they were greatly astonished, saying, "Who then can be saved?" But Jesus looked at them and said, "With man this is impossible, but with God all things are possible.

Luke 16:9-11 (ESV)

And I tell you, make friends for yourselves by means of unrighteous wealth, so that when it fails they may receive you into the eternal dwellings. "One who is faithful in a very little is also faithful in much, and one who is dishonest in a very little is also dishonest in much. If then you have not been faithful in the unrighteous wealth, who will entrust to you the true riches?

Philippians 3:13-14 (NIV)

Brothers and sisters, I do not consider myself yet to have taken hold of it. But one thing I do: Forgetting what is behind and straining toward what is ahead, I press on toward the goal to win the prize for which God has called me heavenward in Christ Jesus.

Luke 9:62 (ESV)

Jesus said to him, "No one who puts his hand to the plow and looks back is fit for the kingdom of God."

1 Thessalonians 5:16-18 (ESV)

Rejoice always, pray without ceasing, give thanks in all circumstances; for this is the will of God in Christ Jesus for you.

Ecclesiastes 7:14 (NIV)

When times are good, be happy; but when times are bad, consider this: God has made the one as well as the other. Therefore, no one can discover anything about their future.

Referenced Scripture

Conclusion

2 Corinthians 11:3 (NIV)

But I am afraid that just as Eve was deceived by the serpent's cunning, your minds may somehow be led astray from your sincere and pure devotion to Christ.

1 Corinthians 10:18-21 (ESV)

Consider the people of Israel: are not those who eat the sacrifices participants in the altar? What do I imply then? That food offered to idols is anything, or that an idol is anything? No, I imply that what pagans sacrifice they offer to demons and not to God. I do not want you to be participants with demons. You cannot drink the cup of the Lord and the cup of demons. You cannot partake of the table of the Lord and the table of demons.

Revelation 12:9 (NIV)

The great dragon was hurled down—that ancient serpent called the devil, or Satan, who leads the whole world astray. He was hurled to the earth, and his angels with him.

Revelation 12:17 (NIV)

Then the dragon was enraged at the woman and went off to wage war against the rest of her offspring—those who keep God's commands and hold fast their testimony about Jesus.

Ephesians 6:11 (ESV)

Put on the whole armor of God, that you may be able to stand against the schemes of the devil.

Revelation 13:7 (NIV)

It was given power to wage war against God's holy people and to conquer them. And it was given authority over every tribe, people, language and nation.

2 Timothy 2:4 (NIV)

No one serving as a soldier gets entangled in civilian affairs, but rather tries to please his commanding officer.

1 John 4:4 (ESV)

Little children, you are from God and have overcome them, for he who is in you is greater than he who is in the world.

Romans 8:31 (ESV)

What then shall we say to these things? If God is for us, who can be against us?

Psalm 145:20 (ESV)

The LORD preserves all who love him, but all the wicked he will destroy.

1 John 2:1 (NIV)

My dear children, I write this to you so that you will not sin. But if anybody does sin, we have an advocate with the Father—Jesus Christ, the Righteous One.

Referenced Textbooks

[3]Alexander, T.D. and Baker, D.W. (2003). *Dictionary of the Old Testament Pentateuch: A compendium of contemporary Biblical scholarship.* pp. 262 & 857

[2]Belsky, J. (2018). *Experiencing the lifespan* (5th ed.). Worth. NY

[1]Schacter, D., Gilbert, D., Wegner, D., and Nock, M. (2020). *Introducing Psychology* (5th ed.). Worth. NY

ABOUT THE AUTHOR

Dr. C.M. Teague is first a Christ follower. He is a faithful worshiper at his local church, in various individual and couple small groups and in his everyday life. His goal is to help bring courage, hope and joy to the lives of others. Dr. Teague is a Doctor of Psychology, and licensed mental health professional. He has an appointment as a faculty member (Lecturer) in psychology at a major public university. Dr. Teague has a private professional counseling practice in which he works with individuals, couples (pre-marital and post-marital) and families and conducts psychosocial mental health testing and assessments. He also conducts research on various topics, which allows his students to gain hands on experience conducting scientific research. Dr. Teague is published in relationship, educational, and trauma related peer review journals. He has written books on marriage, relationships and psychology. Dr. Teague enjoys spending time with his wife and children, reading nonfictional literature, working out and shooting firearms.

Milton Keynes UK
Ingram Content Group UK Ltd.
UKHW022120220724
445848UK00012B/203